GREATEST MOMENTS IN DETROIT
RED WINGS
HISTORY

By Joe Falls, Jerry Green and Vartan Kupelian

Edited by Mike Bynum

From the sports pages of
The Detroit News

SPORTS

The Detroit News

MARK SILVERMAN, Publisher and Editor
JENNIFER CARROLL, Managing Editor
FRANK LOVINSKI, Deputy Managing Editor
PHIL LACIURA, Executive Sports Editor
ALAN WHITT, Deputy Sports Editor
ROB ALLSTETTER, Deputy Sports Editor
CHRISTOPHER KOZLOWSKI, Assistant Managing Editor-Design/Graphics
DAVID KORDALSKI, Design/Graphics Editor
STEVEN FECHT, Director of Photography

RESEARCH ASSISTANCE

Jeff Samoray, Chris Farina, Craig Yuhas, Steve Fecht, Alan Whitt and Rob Allstetter.

ISBN 1-57028-167-X
ISBN (Leatherbound) 1-57028-177-7
Cover Design: Daniel J. Janke, Detroit.
Book Design: Daniel J. Janke and Richard Epps, Detroit.
Typefaces: Concorde BE and Nova, Berkeley Book and Helvetica Condensed.

PUBLISHED BY:

Masters Press
2647 Waterfront Parkway East Drive
Indianapolis, IN 46214
(317) 298-5706

*This book is dedicated
to Vladimir Konstantinov*

CONTENTS

Detroit Bought a Winner,
Then Built an Unforgettable Legacy

Former Victoria Squad Was Foundation for Red Wings

By Jerry Green
The Detroit News

The 1920's were not an ordinary period of time — neither in the world itself nor in the preening, make-believe world of sports.

It was a time when people grabbed at sport heroes, as though there could be any genuine heroism in games a decade after so many nations incurred devastation in a great war.

It was the time of Babe Ruth and Ty Cobb, Jack Dempsey and Gene Tunney and Bill Tilden and Red Grange. These were the athletes who captivated Americans with their sporting domination and with their charisma. Baseball, boxing, football and tennis satisfied the sporting passions of the American public.

But, up in Canada, the citizens were consumed by their sport of ice hockey, a sport they had invented. Canadians grabbed at their own sports figures, transforming them into heroes: Howie Morenz, Nels Stewart, Auriel Joliat, Babe Dye, Cy Denneny and a crusty, red-faced, hot-tempered marksman named Jack Adams.

They played their games in heavy woolen sweaters on gutted sheets of ice in poorly lighted arenas. They wore strange-looking shorts, held up by braces, and leather leg pads beneath woolen stockings. They carried weirdly shaped sticks and played their games on knife-edged skates, at savage speeds.

The exploits of these Canadian athletes were unknown to the ordinary American sports followers who revelled in Ruth's homers and Dempsey's punches and Grange's touchdown runs. Ice hockey was played in Canadian towns such as Toronto, Montreal, Hamilton, Ottawa — the places with franchises in the National Hockey League — and cities out west, such as Vancouver, Victoria. They played for a battered trophy called the Stanley Cup, which once had been dropped-kicked across a frozen canal in Ottawa and forgotten in a snowbank.

In the United States, ice hockey was regarded as an exotic sport, beyond comprehension. It was played by amateurs at a few elite colleges in the East and remote hamlets in northern Michigan and Minnesota, and briefly in the Pacific Northwest by Canadian professionals. But in the middle of the 1920's, cities in the United States started plundering Canadian cities — it would be that way again 70 years later — for franchises in this exotic NHL. First Boston, then Pittsburgh and New York were added as the NHL moved across the border.

American crowds were, at first, apathetic. "... the crowds came to cheer for Canadian teams that played here and the support of the home rooters was almost nonexistent," wrote John McManis in The Detroit News more than a half-century ago. "The crowds were hockeywise, but they reserved their cheers for the Ottawa Senators, the Maple Leafs and the Montreal teams, the Maroons and Les Canadiens."

In Detroit, entrepreneur Charles

Hughes had a brainstorm. Or a pipe dream. He was a reformed sportswriter, a guy who had worked public relations for Teddy Roosevelt. Some of Roosevelt's zest for rugged individualism and bull-moose risk taking seemingly rubbed off.

Hughes was sitting around the Detroit Athletic Club (DAC), gathering place of the city's industrial posh, when he convinced fellow members that Detroit would be a natural location for a pro hockey

Harry (Hap) Holmes, Detroit's first goalie, played on four Stanley Cup championship teams.

WESTERN CHAMPIONS 1924-25

WORLD CHAMPIONS 1924-25

HARRY MEEKING · HAROLD HART · "HAPPY" HOLMES · CLEM LOUGHLIN CAPT · FRANK FREDRICKSON · SLIM HALDERSON · JOCKO ANDERSON

GORDON FRASER · FRANK FOYSTON · MANAGER LESTER PATRICK · JACK WALKER · WALLY ELMER

VICTORIA COUGARS

W.C.H.L. CUP

STANLEY CUP

franchise. After all, a few blocks away, the one-mile narrow Detroit River separated Detroit from Windsor, Michigan from Ontario, the United States from Canada. It was a simple crossing. Bootleggers had been importing Canadian whisky across the river for several years to quench the urges of drinkers in the Prohibition-dry U.S.

Why not bootleg a hockey team to Detroit? All that Detroit lacked was an arena and some hockey players.

Hockey had been imported with some success to other American cities.

"Americans will patronize anything that is spectacular, exciting and thrilling," wrote The Detroit News more than 70 years ago, "and hockey is all of those things."

These were powerfully prosperous times; a good time to finance new franchises. The NHL had placed its first team in the U.S. in 1924-25, the Bruins in Boston. A season later, the NHL added the Pittsburgh Pirates; and the

NHL Hamilton Tigers franchise was exported to New York for a $75,000 fee and renamed the Americans.

As the 1925-26 season opened, the Victoria Cougars were the reigning Stanley Cup champions. Led by Frank Frederickson and coached by Lester Patrick, the Cougars had defeated the Montreal Canadiens, three victories to one, the previous March. Hughes' bright idea was to buy the Cougars from the fragmenting Western League. He collected 73 investors at the DAC.

It was springtime of 1926. Cobb had just started his final season with the Detroit Tigers. And the Cougars had just failed to retain the Stanley Cup in a trans-Canada Final series against the NHL's Montreal Maroons. The Cougars were ripe for plundering, a bootleg job across the border.

On May 15, Hughes and his partners, incorporated as the Detroit Hockey Club, were granted a franchise by the NHL for $100,000. Now they needed players. On Sept. 26, the new team purchased 15 of the Victoria Cougars players. The deal cost them another 100 grand.

They had themselves an NHL franchise. They had 15 skaters. They had a nickname — the Detroit Cougars. Whether they owned a puck at the time is unknown. What is known is that the proprietors of the new NHL Detroit club did not have an ice arena or a place to play their games. They went back across the river to Canada and played home games of their inaugural NHL season in Windsor Arena. They were a team in exile.

The Cougars moved to Detroit/Windsor with an experienced, but aging team. They brought in Harry (Hap) Holmes, the craggy veteran, to play goalie.

Holmes had been goalkeeper on four Stanley Cup championship teams before the trophy became the permanent property of the NHL.

The Cougars had a ready-made scorer in Frank Frederickson, a recognized sharpshooter out West. Also

in the package were such noteworthy players as Clem Laughlin, Slim Halderson, Harry Meeking, Russ Oatman, Jack Walker, Johnny Sheppard (Detroit's first No. 9), Frank Foyston, Hobie Kitchen, Fred Gordon and Harold Hart, who wore No.13.

They were quite a rollicking bunch. Two seasons earlier, as the Victoria Cougars of the Western Hockey League, they had been the core of the Stanley Cup champions. They would remain locked in history 70-plus years later as the last team from outside the NHL to win the Cup.

But, in the autumn of 1926, they were entering the enlarged NHL. Art Duncan, another veteran, was appointed player-coach-general manager. Duncan was a defenseman who had been a true hero. In World War I as a member of the Canadian army, he had won the Military Cross. He had been credited with shooting down 22 German aircraft over the battlefields of France.

The Detroit Cougars were ready to do battle — in their woolen sweaters with an Olde English D, copied from the Tigers, across their chests. With some pomp, they played their first NHL game on Nov. 18, 1926 in Windsor. They lost to the Bruins, 2-0. A few days later, the franchise recorded its first victory, 4-2 over the New York Americans.

Perhaps they were too crusty for their debut in a new league.

Holmes, the goalkeeper, had been

Red Wings Founder

Charles Hughes, a former sportswriter for The Detroit Tribune and the manager of the Detroit Athletic Club, put together a syndicate of investors in 1926 to purchase a professional hockey team and move it to Detroit.

The syndicate purchased the rights to fifteen members of the Victoria Cougars of the Western Hockey League and paid a $100,000 franchise fee to the National Hockey League for the Detroit team.

In 1930, the Detroit Cougars' nickname was changed to the "Falcons" after a newspaper contest.

playing hockey professionally since 1912 when he joined the Toronto Blueshirts of the National Hockey Association. This was five years before the NHL was established. In 1914, Holmes was with the Blueshirts when they won the Stanley Cup over Lester Patrick's Victoria Aristocrats — forerunners of the Cougars.

Patrick was so impressed that when he formed the Pacific Coast Hockey League in 1915, he signed Holmes away from the Blueshirts. It was the start of a hectic decade involving what would be termed free agency 70 years later.

Holmes was assigned to the Seattle Metropolitans, the first major pro team in the United States. With Holmes in goal, the Metropolitans won the Stanley Cup in 1917, defeating the Montreal Canadiens in four games. In three of those games, Holmes outdueled the Canadiens' legendary Georges Vezina.

"The two men were a ready-made contrast for sportswriters," Douglas Hunter wrote in his illustrated history of goaltending, *A Breed Apart*.

"Holmes, who was never seen to crack a smile, was called 'nerveless'; Vezina was 'high-strung.' "

Holmes played his games in a gray baseball cap, in leg pads that looked like protection for cricket players. Goalies of the era did not wear masks, and there were no goalie controver-

sies then. Teams carried one goaltender and he was expected to play every game, unless seriously hurt.

Hap Holmes was a vagabond. After the NHL was organized in 1917, Holmes jumped back across North America. He joined the Toronto Arenas. They won the Stanley Cup that first season — Holmes' third championship and the first for a young blond Toronto forward named Jack Adams. A year later, Holmes was back playing for Seattle.

And, when the Pacific League folded, he went with Lester Patrick to join the Victoria Cougars.

He was with a Cup winner the fourth time in 1925. In 1926, he was the regular goalkeeper for the strug-

After James Norris bought the Detroit team in 1932, the franchise was renamed the Red Wings.

gling, first-season Detroit Cougars, who were playing home games in Windsor's Border Cities Arena.

Frank Frederickson moved to Detroit with the reputation of a prolific scorer. He had been an aviator in the primitive Canadian army air corps during the first World War and lived to talk about a plane crash, according to *Detroit Red Wings: The Illustrated History*, by Richard Bak. Johnny Sheppard was so fixed on

ice that he spent the summer off-season with the midnight sun as a trapper in the Arctic.

Early in the season the Cougars beat the Black Hawks, 1-0. Frederickson scored the lone goal. Holmes, in his gray baseball cap and Olde English D jersey, recorded the shutout. But this was a rare night for the Cougars.

As the season turned into 1927, the Detroit Hockey Club made two

front-office moves that would become patterns for their franchise throughout the ages.

On Jan. 5, they traded away their star player. Frederickson, along with Harry Meeking, was sent to the Bruins for Duke Keats and Archie Briden. And Duncan was removed as coach so he could concentrate on playing defense and serving as general manager. The first Detroit hockey coach had held the job through three vic-

The Red Wings won their first divisional title in 1933-34 and lost to Chicago, 3-1, in the Cup Finals.

tories, 21 defeats and two ties.

Keats, the newcomer from the Bruins, replaced Duncan as a player-coach.

Keats excelled as a player. On March 10, 1927, he scored the new club's first hat trick, against the Pittsburgh Pirates. His career as coach was less distinguished. He managed two victories with seven defeats and two ties over the last 11 games.

At the end of the first season, the Cougars failed to qualify for the Stanley Cup playoffs. They had finished last in the American Division. And their 12-28-4 record was the poorest of the 10 teams in the NHL. John Sheppard was the team's most distinguished player. He led the team in everything, including scoring with 13 goals and eight assists for team-high 21 points,

and penalties with 60 minutes.

The discarded Frederickson helped the Bruins to the Stanley Cup Finals. Boston lost to the Ottawa Senators and their forward/assistant coach, Jack Adams.

The Cougars would move into their million-dollar redbrick Olympia Stadium rink on Grand River Avenue after their first season. It was clearly time for a drastic change, new leadership.

Frank Calder, the president of the NHL, realized that. He contacted Hughes and recommended the hiring of Adams. Adams met with Hughes, his manner brusque and confident.

"You need me more than I need you," he said to Hughes.

It was true.

Hughes hired Adams as coach and general manager of the Cougars. He would remain in the employ of the Detroit Hockey Club for 35 years.

Adams had a rough, typical roustabout hockey background. He was born in Fort William, Ontario, in 1895, son of a locomotive engineer on the railroad.

He bought his first ice skates as a lad from the proceeds of selling newspapers in saloons. In his youth, he went to work in the grain elevators.

"I worked for 10 hours a day for 22 cents an hour," he recalled once.

Those two early experiences gave him two lifelong principles — abstinence from drinking alcohol and a tight-fisted appreciation for money.

Adams went off to play hockey

at Calumet in the Northern Michigan League against lumberjacks and miners. Soon, he was a professional with the Toronto Arenas, then Vancouver, back to Toronto with the St. Pat's and then to Ottawa for a last-hurrah as a player with the Senators.

He had a job to do selling hockey to Detroit. Despite the new Olympia in 1927, the home team was booed by the bulk of the fans who crossed the river from Ontario to watch their national pastime in the United States.

"It was the first place I ever saw that the home team wasn't popular," Adams said years later. "The crowds used to come out to see us lose. We were a new team in this part of the country and we weren't popular. The crowd in Detroit was mostly Canadian and the Canadians had their favorites. They had always followed the fortunes of the established teams and they wanted to see them win. It wasn't strange for us to get a good jeering for knocking off one of the well-known teams."

Gradually, the Cougars developed a fan base. Adams was a wheeler-dealer.

He made nine deals his first season. In their third season, 1928-29, the Cougars made the playoffs for the first time. Then they missed again — and the Cougars heeded the power of the media.

The local papers suggested that the Detroit Hockey Club could change its luck by changing its name. The Cougars then became the Fal-

Ebbie Goodfellow's 25 goals in 1930-31 set a Detroit scoring record that was not broken for 14 years.

cons, but the luck hardly improved. In the summer of 1932, with the Depression slugging Detroit, the pipe-dream management had to sell out.

The franchise was purchased by Jim Norris, an industrialist with roots in Montreal. As a boy, Norris, had played for a team named the Winged

Wheelers in the Montreal Athletic Association. The club's insignia was a wheel with a wing attached. Perfect for Detroit, said Jim Norris. And the name of the Detroit Hockey team was changed again, to the Red Wings — to challenge the vagaries and quirks of history.

COUGARS STICKS CRUSH PIRATES

Detroit Outshoots Pittsburgh, 41-33, in Team Effort

By Harold M. George

Special to The Detroit News

The Detroit Cougars' 7-1 victory over the Pittsburgh Pirates last night brought about one change in the standings of teams in the American Division of the National Hockey League.

In games won and lost Detroit remains at the bottom, but the Cougars forged ahead of the Pirates in number of goals

PIRATES

1

COUGARS

7

Detroit,
March 10, 1927

scored for the season. They also reached within eight goals of the number scored by the New York Rangers. Detroit now has a total of 65 goals, Pittsburgh has 60 and the Rangers 73.

The Cougars employed nearly every method in hockey last night to amass their seven goals. They scored on lone plays, on rebounds, on double and single passes and on caroms from the boards. Everything worked for

them. Each goal was scored in a different way. Eight players figured in the seven goals.

Three of Detroit's goals followed an unusual practice in substitutions. On three occasions, Detroit replaced its whole team, except the goaler, with other players. A goal came almost immediately after each one of these wholesale substitutions.

Keats, who scored three of the Cougars' goals, got the first early in the first period by clever stick handling. He dodged through the Pittsburgh defense. He got the second

The 1926-27 Detroit Cougars were forced to play at Windsor's Border Cities Arena.

10 minutes later. Darragh, the Pirate wing, in a rush toward the Detroit goal, slammed head-on into Duncan and lost the puck. Keats seized it, stopped to look back at the fallen gladiators and then skated unopposed to the Pirate goal.

Pittsburgh got its only goal late in the first period. Holmes stopped Darragh's shot, but Langlois caught the rebound and plugged it in before Holmes could get set.

Gordon scored Detroit's third goal early in the second period. Keats passed to Sheppard in back of the Pittsburgh net. Sheppard, instead of trying for a goal himself, passed back toward center ice to Gordon, who caught it and sent it crashing back.

The fourth Detroit score was unearned. Loughlin went into the goal and Worters, the Pirate goaler, came out to meet him. Loughlin shot the puck to Foyston, who had skated in behind Worters. Foyston was off-side. It was almost a straight-for-

ward pass. But referee Jerry LaFlamme allowed the score.

Keats scored again in the second period. Gordon shot the puck against the back boards and Keats caught it as it came out the other side of the net. He beat Worters easily. Walker went in alone for his score, Detroit's sixth, in the third period. An entire new Detroit team then took the ice, and Briden got by the Pittsburgh defense, scoring unassisted.

SETTING PERFECT BUT COUGARS LOSE

Ottawa's Champions Spoil First Game in Detroit

By H.G. Salsinger

Special to The Detroit News

Detroit saw her first game of major hockey last night and, while it was deluxe presentation, it was not a highly satisfactory one from a Detroit point of view, with the world champions from Ottawa defeating Detroit, 2-1.

Still, it was a colorful occasion. Major John W. Smith presented chrysanthemums to Jack Adams, the new manager of the Cougars, the University of Michigan band played and also yelled in true collegiate manner, and, between periods, Norval Baptie and Gladys Lamb presented a program of figure skating. The side features were pleasing, even if the result of the game was not.

Detroit was represented by a team in the National Hockey League all last season, but the games were played in Windsor whenever the schedule called for a home appearance. The first time

OTTAWA

2

COUGARS

1

Detroit,
Nov. 22, 1927

the team ever competed on Detroit ice was last night, and a jammed house saw the game. Every seat was sold before 7:20 and after that what standing room could be disposed of was soon gone.

Ottawa presented practically the same lineup that won the world title for the Dominion city last spring. Of the regulars of last year, only the hard-going Hooley Smith was missing. But Frank Finnigan, playing the wing that the effervescent Hooley looked after last year, did fairly well. He proved a capable successor.

Detroit scored her goal in the first period and she held the one-point lead going into the second period. But in this stretch of play Ottawa tied the count, and, in the final period, the champions scored the deciding goal.

Detroit's goal in the opening period was scored after 10 minutes of play. It followed a number of rushes. On two of these, Hay distinguished himself with shots

that gave Connell trouble. Each was a difficult save. Finally, Sheppard and Keats went down together. Keats' shot was stopped by Connell, but Johnny Sheppard, getting the puck on the rebound, beat Connell from in front of two rushing defensemen.

Finnigan was the most aggressive player that the world champions showed in this period. He tested Holmes' defensive skill with three hard shots and, with four minutes to go, Nighbor, the veteran center of the Ottawa team, broke through Detroit's first line and skated to the net.

The Detroit defense, falling back, converged at the net. Four players, including Holmes, the goaltender, tumbled in a heap in the mouth of the net, and Nighbor, skating into the heap, shoved the puck through the mass and into the net with his skate, an offside. It was the best chance Ottawa had through the period.

Ottawa started a mass attack with the start of the second period. Nighbor, Clancy and Kilrea were in Detroit ice, shooting wildly most of the time and giving Holmes few stops, but finally Nighbor broke through and beat the veteran Detroit goaler with a beautifully timed shot.

A moment later, Kilrea, taking a pass from Clancy, gave Holmes an opportunity to make a spectacular stop.

With the score tied, Ottawa fell back on defense. Aurie, shooting at a difficult angle, forced Connell to a difficult save. Clancy rode in on Holmes, but Holmes stopped Sheppard on a pass from Keats, pulled one that brought up the crowd but that brought no score. Clancy twice came streaking down the ice only to be stopped at the net. A solo rush by Walker ended in a wild shot.

Connell beat Noble on a shot that would ordinarily score. Noble had come the length of the ice alone. Walker, Sheppard and Brown went down together. Then Sheppard and Cooper.

But they found the Ottawa defense too good. Then Brown, Sheppard and Cooper, going down in a line, pulled Connell from the net, but the Ottawa defense fell back and checked the rush before the Detroit line could recover a loose puck. Keats, going alone, missed a dead shot. Kilrea and A. Smith broke through the Detroit defense and skated in on Holmes, only to be beaten at the net. This play ended a torrid 20 minutes of battling.

At the start of the last period,

The 1927-28 Cougars returned to Detroit after Olympia Stadium was completed. The Cougars finished with a record of 19-19-6.

Connell stopped a long shot from Hay and another one from Cooper. Nighbor furnished Holmes with a chance for a spectacular save. Kilrea drove a long one into Holmes' chest. Connell made a fine save on an angle shot from Cooper. Four Cougars sprawled in the mouth of the net and broke up an Ottawa charge. Nighbor was leading the Ottawa offensive, but was forced to shoot from long range.

Holmes stopped one from Kilrea with the blades of his skates. Walker, taking the puck along the boards, passed to Sheppard, in front of the Ottawa net, but Sheppard shot wide. A moment later, Finnigan and Nighbor made a rush for the Detroit net.

Finnigan took the pass from Nighbor and sent the puck flashing between Holmes' legs for the second Ottawa goal.

Keats, Cooper and Noble got through the Ottawa defense lines, but Connell beat the attack by throwing himself across the ice, stopping the puck with his body. He made a fine save on an angle shot by J. Sheppard. The Cougars were going down in lines of fours, trying desperately for a score. Ottawa, gaining possession of the puck, would stall along, bringing hoots from the crowd, but the defensive measure worked. The Cougars could not break through, and the one-point margin of the champions survived.

FALCONS BECOME SENSATION OF LEAGUE

Detroit Holds Second Place in American Division

By Lloyd Northard

Special to The Detroit News

The Detroit Falcons, counted out of the race by the experts before the National Hockey League season started, today hold second place in the American Division, the highest position the Falcons have occupied in two seasons.

Only one point ahead of Chicago and leading the Boston Bruins by four points, the Falcons, with 8 games to play, appear certain of entering the Stanley Cup playoffs for the second time.

A piece of the Blarney Stone under goaler "Flat" Walsh's chest pads, the assistance of the two weakest officials seen at Olympia this season and the combined skating, holding and slashing efforts of the Montreal Maroons weren't enough to stop the Falcons Sunday night. They continued their unbroken string of successful endeavors on their home ice, running their string to 18 successive games in which they haven't been beaten, with a 2-1 victory.

Two weeks ago, a young Irish miss who gave only the name of Kathleen came to the Maroons dressing room in Montreal and asked an attendant to give a fragment of stone to Walsh. She said to tell him it was a piece of the original Blarney Stone. Her family had a piece of the stone, and she had taken this little bit to bring good luck to the Maroons' goaler.

MAROONS

1

FALCONS

2

Detroit,
Feb. 28. 1932

The luck charm worked perfectly in the first game, and Walsh scored one of the few shutouts of his career. Since then it hasn't functioned as the Maroons have been beaten by both Chicago and Detroit. The charm didn't help Walsh's flow or oratory either for he couldn't convince goal judge Archie Connors or the officials that the Falcons' winning goal wasn't in the net. After digging the puck from behind him with his stick, Walsh joined Lionel Conacher and Archie Wilcox in a waste or words trying to have the goal called back.

George Mallinson, who comes from the same city as the Maroons and whose handling of games has been protested frequently this season, and Jack Cameron of Toronto, who has had little experience handling professional hockey games, were the officials.

Bobby Hewitson, one of the oldest and one of the best referees to handle games in the league in the past five years, watched two periods of the game from the press box. Then Hewitson left. Most of the more than 7,000 spectators wished that Mallinson and Cameron had been the ones to go and had left Hewitson to handle the last period as a hockey game should be conducted.

Just why a referee from the same city as one of the contesting teams should be named to handle a game while a far better referee from a neutral city was allowed to sit on the bench only President Frank Calder can explain. The

Maroons were supposedly weakened through the loss of Nelson Stewart and Hooley Smith, but they were strengthened through the addition of their fellow townsman, Mallinson.

When Cameron blew his whistle to end play after the Falcons' second goal, the Maroons continued to try to rush the puck.

Mallinson saw that Cameron had stopped play, but he refused to blow his whistle to stop the bumping players and play continued for a full minute while Cameron was talking to the goal judge. Cameron had to skate among the players and blow his whistle again to stop play.

Johnny Sorrell scored the winning goal. The lean left winger has been an opportunist with his goals on Olympia ice this season. It was Sorrell that scored the goal that broke the tie and brought the Falcons their first home victory of the season over the Maroons.

He placed the Falcons in the lead over Les Canadiens in their first game here. His goal beat the Toronto Maple Leafs 3-2 in overtime, and he drove in the goal that tied Chicago and helped the Falcons go on to win, 3-1.

Olympia Stadium, built in 1927, could accommodate crowds of more than 15,000. It would be the home of the Red Wings for 52 years.

BRUNETEAU WINS NHL'S LONGEST GAME

Detroit Goaler Smith Stops 91 Shots

By Sam Greene

Special to The Detroit News

Thanks to a goal by Modere Bruneteau, the Detroit Red Wings stand today with a one-game edge over the Montreal Maroons in the annual series for the National Hockey League championship.

With a Frank Merriwell touch and one sweep of a hockey stick, Bruneteau qualified as one of the heroes of the professional sport by scoring a goal after two hours and 56 ½ minutes of battling in The Forum last night. He tallied on a short pass from Hector Kilrea to give the Wings a 1-0 victory and put an end to the longest game in history of organized hockey — nearly six hours of actual time.

After finishing the customary hour of competition, the two clubs began an overtime struggle that in

RED WINGS
1
———
MAROONS
0
Montreal,
March 24, 1936

itself lasted an hour and 56 ½ minutes, breaking the all-time endurance record set by Toronto and Boston in a similar series three years ago.

On the night of April 3, 1933, Toronto played a total of two hours 44 minutes and 46 seconds before Ken Doraty, now of Cleveland, broke the scoreless deadlock with a shot that beat Tiny Thompson. The teams were in their sixth extra period when Doraty drove the puck into the Boston cage.

Detroit and Montreal likewise were in the sixth 20-minute overtime session last night when Bruneteau connected. Both clubs had tried valiantly for almost three hours to find the range. Norman Smith, in the Detroit goal, had kicked out 91 shots, and Lorne Chabot, the Montreal goaler, had turned aside 66.

It looked as if the tie would stand interminably. At every turn, the defense had overmatched the attack. There had been brilliant and

Wings' goalie Normie Smith shut out the Maroons for 248 minutes and 32 seconds in the Cup semifinals.

concerted rushes that seemed certain to succeed, only to fail at the goal mouth.

With the playoff overtime periods lasting 20 minutes instead of the usual 10-minute overtime periods of the regular season, players of both sides were plainly tired. Spectators were asking each other why Jack Adams and Tommy Gorman did not get together and call a halt.

"Call it no contest. Call it a draw. Call it anything but get it over." That was the general attitude of the thinning crowd that earlier in the evening had numbered 10,000 — the largest of the winter in Montreal.

Frank Calder, the President of the league, was sitting in a box along the rail.

Hec Kilrea turned to him and half-jokingly inquired why he did not stop the game. Calder said nothing and obviously had no intention of acting.

It was less than a minute later that Kilrea decided to do something about the situation himself. He seized the puck inside his own defense, after a scramble with Maroon players, and raced down the middle lane. He started to split the defense, then consisting of Allan Shields and Cyclone Wentworth. He changed his mind and swerved to his left.

There was Bruneteau, the youngest of the Wings in experience, the stripling from Winnipeg who was promoted from the Olympics only a few weeks ago.

Kilrea passed the puck to Bruneteau, and the rookie caught it squarely on the stick. He was on the left of the goaler, less than 12 feet from the net. Half the cage was wide open, but Bruneteau shot for the side that was almost closed. By luck or marksmanship, or both, he sent the puck past Chabot. The big Frenchman did not touch it. Perhaps he did not see it.

The goal judge was so surprised, or so sleepy, that it seemed half a minute before he flashed the red light behind Chabot. The game was over.

The Red Wings massed at mid-ice to pat Bruneteau on the back. They almost pulled the red jersey off his frail body. They half carried him to the dressing room, where Bruneteau was so excited he could hardly talk.

"Where did you get the puck from?" he was asked.

"I don't know," said Bruneteau. "All I know is I hope my old man is listening to the radio. I showed 'em they didn't bring me up for nothing this time."

The Red Wings' locker room was bedlam. Everybody was trying to talk at once. Nobody paid any attention to the praise Jack Adams was handing out to his squad, with particular reference to Norman Smith.

Montreal critics had pictured Smith as the weak link in the Detroit machine. They had said the Wings could not win with him in the net. They agreed that Detroit had speed, power and punch in the premier line of Larry Aurie, Herbie Lewis and Marty Berry. They did not discount the efficiency of Douglas Young, Bucko McDonald and Ebbie Goodfellow in the rear guard. They cited Syd Howe, Johnny Sorrell and the Kilrea brothers as worthy of championship rating, but Smith, they argued, lacked poise, experience. He would crack under the drain of a championship setting.

Well, Smith did nothing of the sort. He was appearing in his first major-league playoff and he deserves a place above even that of Bruneteau when credit for the Wings' victory is being allotted.

No goaler could have done a better job than Smith. He made miraculous saves in every period. He fended off shots with his stick, his glove, his pads. He sprawled on the ice time and again, smothering the puck beneath him. When the Wings were shorthanded and the Maroons swarmed in on him with the power play, Smith checked every thrust. He caused Wilfred Cude to exclaim: "I never saw goaltending like that."

Chabot matched Smith's brilliance until Bruneteau spoiled his evening. The veteran Frenchman was up and down, moving from post to post, kicking out pucks from every angle. The one he missed was not better timed than ones he blocked, but there must be an end to everything.

All of the excitement, of course, did not concern Bruneteau's goal, but that is what mostly matters. It provided a dramatic finish by a recruit in his second year of professional hockey and his first major playoff.

Bruneteau joined the Detroit Olympics last year and was elevated to the Wings at the start of the present season. He was lacking in experience and sent back to the International League club.

A few weeks ago, when the Red Wings encountered a long slump on the road, Jack Adams called for Bruneteau. He has been playing part time on the third line that otherwise consists of Wallie Kilrea and Johnny Sorrell.

While Bruneteau gave the Wings their winning goal last night, other players contributed heavily to their success. Bucko McDonald, likewise a newcomer in playoff competition, enhanced his reputation of being the hardest checking defenseman in the National League. Time after time, he knocked Maroons to the ice with perfectly legal checks.

In the first period, both Dave Trottier and Shields of the Maroons were in the penalty box at the same time. But the Wings could not profit by their advantage in man power though they tried every device within their knowledge. Once they had five forwards inside the Montreal blue line but could not score.

In the second period, Hec Kilrea was penalized for tripping Russ Bilnco, but the Maroons made only futile rushes on the Detroit goal during his absence. There was the same result, or lack of it, in the third period when Wallie Kilrea was in the penalty box. Chabot, impatient over

Jack Adams

the failure of the Montreal forwards, beat his pad with his stick and pleaded for a goal — but without reward.

The regulation 60 minutes finished, and the overtime started. It became monotonous to the spectators as the rival forces sailed up and down the ice in a vain effort to break the tie.

Some of the crowd started to leave. Others ordered coffee and drank it in their seats. Wives explained facetiously that they had to go home to prepare breakfast. A wit suggested that the teams flip a coin to settle the issue. Another countered with the idea that they decide the ownership of the Stanley Cup in the same fashion.

It was even less fun for the men on the ice. They were tiring under the grind. Adams ordered hot tea for the Wings, and it was served during the 10-minute intermissions.

The first three overtime periods passed without a penalty. Then Hooley Smith was sentenced for two minutes.

In the fifth overtime session, Hooley Smith held up the game for a prolonged argument with Referee Ag Smith. The Maroons' center contended that the official should not have blown his whistle to stop play when the puck was in Maroon possession behind the Detroit cage. The referee answered that the puck was "frozed" to the boards. Spectators took sides with Hooley and rained all manner of trash on the playing surface. A crew of sweepers came on to clear the debris, and play was resumed.

When the sixth overtime period started, Herbie Lewis skated over to the press box and inquired: "We aren't keeping you boys up, are we?"

The Wings were beginning to feel the uplifting effects of the hot tea. The crowd, having consulted the program, was hoping that the game would last five more minutes and thereby break the all-time record for duration. By this time, they apparently did not care which side won.

The game dragged on, not for five minutes but for 16 before Bruneteau brought it to a rousing close and made the Wings favorites for the National League title. It was then 2:35.

RED WINGS NEAR CUP AFTER ROUT OF MAPLE LEAFS

Detroit Sets Modern Scoring Record

By Lloyd Northard

Special to The Detroit News

After spending hours delving into records, Detroit hockey followers this morning reached two definite conclusions: First — the Red Wings have a death grip on the Stanley Cup. Second — the Red Wings have established a new scoring record for Stanley Cup games in modern hockey by defeating the Toronto Maple Leafs 9-4 at Olympia Tuesday night before 12,456 happy spectators.

No team ever has lost the Stanley Cup after winning the first two games of the series. Today the Wings are resting in Toronto, confident they can bring the 43-year-old world hockey championship trophy back to Detroit with them Friday. They boarded a train after midnight.

While the Wings never have won the Stanley Cup, one would have thought nearing its possession was a custom with them as they leisurely prepared to leave for Toronto

MAPLE LEAFS

4

RED WINGS

9

Detroit,
April 7, 1936

Tuesday night. Their dressing room was quieter and more orderly than after most of the games in the regular schedule. There was no tension, no celebration.

Perhaps the ease with which they dropped the puck back of George Hainsworth through three periods had taken the thrill out of the "crucial" game. For the second successive time, they had outskated, outchecked and outrifled the Leafs. They saw nothing ahead but speedy possession of the Stanley Cup. The Cup has arrived in Toronto from Montreal and is waiting only another Detroit victory for the official presentation to its possessors for a year's tenure.

The present National Hockey League was formed in 1917. Records since that time show the highest score ever made by a team in a Stanley Cup game was seven goals, the Toronto Arenas winning from Montreal Canadiens, 7-3. In 1932, the Toronto Maple Leafs scored six goals in each of three successive games

against the New York Rangers.

Tuesday night, a man sat at the rinkside who had helped pile up those seven goals for the Arenas back in the spring of 1918. Yet, he smiled broadly as the Wings equalled the mark of his old teammates in the third period and his smile grew broader as they drove home two more goals to set the new mark. He is John James Adams, now manager of the Red Wings and right wing for the Arenas in the first year of the National Hockey League.

Realizing a second successive victory for Detroit would be all but the finishing blow to their Stanley Cup hopes, the Leafs played open hockey, seeking to get the jump. But instead the first period was an exact duplicate of the first game Sunday night. Before the Leafs could get settled the Wings had taken the lead. In 10 minutes, they had a three-goal lead and they increased their margin in each of the next two periods.

When a hockey club scores nine goals it has to be a team victory. All but three of the Wings had a part in the scoring.

The Red Wings set a Stanley Cup scoring record in their 9-4 win over Toronto in the Finals.

Billy Thoms, "Buzz" Boll and Bob Davidson each scored a goal and an assist for the Leafs. Joe Primeau pushed in Toronto's other goal, while Jack Shill, Harvey Jackson and Frank Finnigan had assists.

Wally Kilrea started the record scoring and rout of the Leafs after a minute and a half of play when he raced, unchecked, through the Toronto defense to drive the rebound of Sorrell's shot past Hainsworth. A change of lines brought Barry on the ice to score his first goal. Bowman drew Hainsworth out of his net and passed backward to Barry, who counted in the open cage. Frank Clancy drew the first penalty, and the Wings attacked with five forwards, Lewis picking the puck out of

Hainsworth's lap after Sorrell's shot to give the Wings a three-goal lead.

Boll cut the lead by scoring from Thoms' pass as Smith was falling, trying to stop his shot. McDonald came out of the penalty box at the exact second to join Hec Kilrea in a rush that distanced all the Leafs, and Bucko pushed the puck between Hainsworth's feet.

"Red" Horner's second penalty opened the way for the Wings to start scoring in the second period. Sorrell was on the receiving end of a double pass by Barry and Howe. He pivoted to pull Hainsworth out and then scored behind him. Howe made a backward pass as he passed the net and Pettinger pushed it into the corner of the cage. Primeau squeezed

Shill's pass between Smith's right foot and the post for Toronto's second goal.

Five goals were scored in the third period. Sorrell started it by beating Hainsworth with a snap shot off left wing. Thoms beat Smith with a low shot. Hainsworth stalled with a loose puck behind his net. Hec Kilrea racked in, checked the goaler and took the puck. Pettinger raced up center ice and lifted the puck into the cage before Hainsworth could shuffle back.

Davidson's shot climbed over Smith's outstretched leg for the Leafs' last goal, and McDonald ended the scoring by taking the puck from Andy Blair at the Leafs' blue line and skating in to lift the puck over the Toronto goaler as he made a desperate dive to cover the open corner.

RED WINGS WIN FIRST STANLEY CUP

More Than 14,000 See Clincher in Gardens

By Lloyd Northard

Special to The Detroit News

Detroit's 10-year quest for the world's hockey championship ended successfully and sensationally tonight in Maple Leaf Gardens.

Fighting off another desperate third-period attack by the Toronto Maple Leafs, Jack Adams' amazing Red Wings closed the 1936 Stanley Cup series with a 3-2 victory before one of the largest crowds ever to see a hockey game.

There were more that 14,000 spectators on their feet at the finish.

Half an hour after the game ended, James Norris Sr., and Adams were presented with the 42-year-old historic trophy by Frank Calder, the President of the National Hockey League, in Calder's hotel room. For Norris, it represented an ambition of years. Not until four years ago was he able to purchase a National Hockey League team and he has bent every effort to building a championship team.

RED WINGS

3

MAPLE LEAFS

2

Toronto,
April 11, 1936

This afternoon the Red Wings will return home bringing the Stanley Cup. They were permitted to remain here overnight to celebrate the biggest night in their hockey careers. With both the Prince of Wales and Stanley Cups now in their possession, the Wings' trophy case at Olympia will have to be enlarged.

The Wings are the first team to win both the National Hockey League and Stanley Cup championships since 1931 when the Montreal Canadiens were double champions. It also marked the fifth time in the 10 years Detroit has been in the National League that an American city has won the Stanley Cup.

The final game of the Detroit-Toronto series was the closest and hardest fought. The Wings, anxious to make up for their slips on defense that cost them the third game here Thursday, were determined to prove it had caused only a delay of two nights. The Leafs, spurred by a victory after two one-sided defeats, were equally determined to force the series

into a fifth game at Detroit Tuesday.

For the first time in the series, the Leafs were first to lead. In each of the first three games, the Wings had scored three goals before Toronto could score. With less than two minutes to play in the first period, Joe Primeau raced down right wing, swung back of "Bucko" McDonald, and made a perfect shot just inside the post to Normie Smith's right.

At the halfway mark in the second period, Ebbie Goodfellow scored his first goal and first point of the playoff series. He broke fast from his own defense zone and passed to Johnny Sorrell on left wing, drawing the Leafs' defense. The return pass was perfect and so was Goodfellow's delayed shot to tie the score.

In less than a minute, the Wings were in the lead. Barry headed the rush and gave Lewis a quick short pass inside the Leafs' blue line. Lewis made a perfect pass that allowed Barry time enough to draw George Hainsworth out of position and pitch the puck into the wide open net.

Pete Kelly was the only Wing who hadn't gained a scoring point

Pete Kelly, who became one of the Red Wings' all-time greats, scored a goal in the third period.

in the series and joined the scoring ranks in the third period. Lewis again made the pass to the end of Kelly's stick, and the red-headed right winger lifted the puck over Hainsworth's left shoulder. The goal light didn't flash, but referee Bill Stewart immediately allowed the goal. The goal judge reported after the game that the light failed to flash on when he snapped the switch. He said there was no question of it being a perfect goal and that he had waved to Stewart when the light failed.

The Leafs continued their contin-ual rushing with five forwards. Smith never performed more sensationally. He appeared to be all arms and legs.

Finally the Leafs broke through, Billy Thoms, one of the fastest skaters in the league, broke away, distanc-ing the tired Wing forwards and came straight at Smith. His shot was aimed for the corner at Smith's right. The Detroit goaler dived but the puck suddenly turned on edge and rolled over Smith's outstretched legs.

But the Wings didn't drop back inside their blue line with only a one-goal lead as they did Thursday night. They attacked as often as the Leafs and had more scoring chances in the last five minutes, but Hainsworth was unbeatable.

The crowd was announced as 14,728 paid customers.

Jack Adams changed his starting lineup, opening for the first time with his second line of Gordon Pettinger, Syd Howe and Hec Kilrea against the Leafs' second line. Hec Kilrea was first to have a shot at Hainsworth from off right wing. Horner tripped Howe, and the Wings attacked with five for-wards, Sorrell and Howe joining the

first line of Barry, Aurie and Lewis. Hainsworth turned Aurie's shot to the boards. Lewis had a fine scoring chance but shot wide, the puck going outside the post to Hainsworth's left.

The Leafs' first line finally made Smith stop a shot, Harvey Jackson shooting from just outside the Detroit blue line. Conacher then swung around McDonald, but couldn't beat Smith from six feet out. On the return rush, Hainsworth saved from Barry.

Smith turned aside another long shot from H. Jackson and again Barry came back to bounce a shot off Hainsworth's chest. Conacher tried to break through the Detroit defense but was stopped, and his shot was wide. Close checking kept both teams shooting from outside the blue line until "Pep" Kelly raced in on right wing but his drive hit the side of the cake. Finnigan shook Smith with a low drive off right wing. Howe broke up a fast rush by Boll. Blair appeared dangerous, but the puck was called back for offside.

There was no advantage for either team in the first half of the period.

Conacher drove a hard shot across the front of the net. Lewis was well inside the Leaf blue line but delayed his shot too long and it was blocked. Barry rolled a shot off right

Larry Aurie scored 147 goals for the Red Wings in his career. His number (6) has never been worn since his retirement.

wing. Young drove a shot from just outside the blue line as the whistle sounded for an offside. Hainsworth missed the shot completely, the puck diving under his arm and into the net, but the goal was called back.

Kelly broke away fast down right wing, but his shot from the boards passed harmlessly across the front of the net. Day drew a penalty box for holding Wally Kilrea in front of the Leafs' net. Again the Wings sent out the "power" line. Blair hooked the puck from Howe and raced down right wing. He passed to Finnigan, who returned the pass inside the Detroit blue line. Smith made a diving save of Blair's shot just inside the post, and Hainsworth had to move fast to keep Aurie's shot out of the net.

Joe Primeau stole the puck from a Detroit rush inside his own blue line. He bounced the puck off the boards to get around the Detroit forwards and easily circled McDonald. He turned across the goal mouth and beat Smith with a shot just inside the post at 18:11.

Howe then broke through the Leafs' defense. He was tripped as he started his shot 10 feet out. He went sliding into the net, upsetting Hainsworth. Hec Kilrea raced in and the red light flashed, but Ag Smith ruled the puck had rolled into the net off Howe's chest. Smith had no explanations of why he did not award Detroit a penalty shot or why no Toronto man was penalized. During the last minute and a half, the Leafs lifted the puck down the ice.

Primeau's goal marked the first time the Leafs have taken the lead in four games with the Wings. In each of the first three games, Detroit has scored three goals before the Leafs could count.

Smith turned out Day's long shot ticketed for the corner. Clancy tipped Howe's pass off Hec Kilrea's stick in front of the Toronto net. Hainsworth made two saves off Howe in less than a minute. Conacher twice missed the net shooting off right wing. Then he was wide off right wing and wide off the other wing. Conacher took three punches at Goodfellow after Ebbie had poke checked the puck off Conacher's stick. Both were given penalties.

Howe went off on the next play for tripping Boll. Then Young broke away alone and was tripped from behind by Blair. Again no penalty shot was called. Lewis just missed Pettinger's pass in front of the Leafs' net, and Smith saved from Davidson. Primeau fell as he raced into the Detroit goal mouth. He was knocked out when his head hit the goal post.

Thoms was well inside the Wings' blue line, but his hard shot was wide of the post. Goodfellow just poked the puck away from Art Jackson three feet in front of the Wing cage. Then he turned and rushed down center ice. At the Toronto blue line he passed to Sorrell, who returned the pass about 15 feet out, Goodfellow pivoted around Clancy and, after stalling with the puck, didn't give Hainsworth a chance with an open corner shot. It was Goodfellow's first point in the playoffs. Back on even terms, the Wings took command of the play. Barry started down center, cut over to left wing and gave Lewis a short pass. Herbie returned in, and Barry raced in unchecked to feint Hainsworth to the short side and scored in the far corner. In less than a minute, Aurie missed scoring by inches and Hainesworth had trouble clearing the puck.

Thoms' shot was straight at Smith. Then Boll sent in a troublesome roller. Goodfellows' pass deep in the Leaf defense zone was off the tip of Hec Kilrea's stick. Thoms split the Detroit defense and was through all alone. Smith made a long dive to turn in the most sensational save of the game as Thoms spilled over him. Smith had to dive to smother a looping shot by Art Jackson. The Leafs outplayed the Wings' third line by a wide margin, Smith having a busy three minutes to keep the Leafs from evening the count.

With a change of line, Conacher drove another of his low shots at Smith who had it covered all the way. Harvey Jackson's passout hit Goodfellow's skate and Smith had to jump to keep the puck out of the net. Conacher just missed the corner after circling the Detroit net.

Howe had the first shot of the third period from center ice, Pettinger followed with another long one. Thoms lifted the puck over the Detroit net. Smith made another sensational save and cleared by batting the puck high in the air when Boll skated around and didn't shoot until three feet out.

Hainsworth then saved smartly from Howe at the other end and had to repeat off Pettinger, Barry and Bowman rushed, the play ending with the puck in the side of the Leafs' cage.

Goodfellow's stick just missed Barry's pass in the Leafs' goal mouth with Hainsworth off balance. Smith saved from Conacher after he had circled the Detroit net. Primeau had an open net from the rebound but shot outside the post. Smith leaped far to his right and just tipped out Primeau's low shot.

Barry's clever hook checking at center ice kept the Leafs from getting their attack started. With 13 minutes to play Toronto sent five forwards out. The Wings' third line faced them. Young broke with the puck and Wally Kilrea bounced a backhand off Hainsworth's pads. Smith again made a brilliant save of Boll's shot and Sorrell returned with a high shot off Hainsworth's chest.

The Wings weren't holding the puck against the boards as they did Thursday night. The were driving it down the ice. Then the Wings broke up a Leaf rush. Lewis gave Pete Kelly a perfect pass and Kelly earned his first point of the playoff by lifting the puck over Hainsworth's left shoulder. The goal judge didn't flash the light but referee Stewart allowed the goal against the protests of the Leafs.

Smith was all arms and legs for the next two minutes. He made three rapid saves that had the crowd screaming. Hec Kilrea missed a good chance when in alone on Hainsworth.

Then Thoms rushed alone, outguessed Bowman and beat Smith with a shot that jumped over his legs.

Horner came in fast to take a pass but his shot rolled outside the post. The Leafs maintained a constant rushing attack while the Wings were lifting the puck at every chance. Smith buried Primeau's shot in his pads. Young was away alone but shot over the Leafs' net. Barry was away all alone but Hainesworth outguessed him with a fine one-handed save.

"Pep" Kelly shot wide of the net. McDonald spilled Conacher hard as he was leading a rush. Smith saved from Davidson and lost his stick. The Wings averted danger when Pete Kelly rolled the puck over the blue line. Howe, Kelly and Wally Kilrea worried the Leafs in their zone. Hainsworth had to jump to save Howe's shot and then leap again for the rebound. Wally Kilrea was in for a hard shot, and again Rowe tested Hainsworth from the rebound.

There was a minute and a half to play when the Wings got an offside at the Leafs' blue line. There was only a minute when there was another face off to the left of the Leafs' net. Aurie checked Boll near the Detroit net and drove the puck the length of the rink. There was 10 seconds when the Leafs rushed but an offside followed with two seconds to play. The finishing bell pealed out a victory song for the Wings as Goodfellow rushed back to kiss Smith and "King" Clancy of the Leafs followed with a big hug.

WINGS FIRST AMERICAN TEAM TO REPEAT CUP WIN

Rangers Fall, 3-0, in Fifth, Decisive Game

By John McManis

Special to The Detroit News

Hockey's championship banners still fly high in Detroit.

The Detroit Red Wings, battered by all the game's winds of adversity and wrecked half a dozen times by major injuries, retained their world championship of hockey when they defeated the New York Rangers, 3-0, at Olympia Thursday in the fifth and deciding game of the Stanley Cup Finals. A crowd of 14,102, biggest of the playoffs crowds in Detroit, saw the game.

It was the second Stanley Cup championship for the Red Wings in two years. The Red Wings won the National Hockey League title last year and this.

Only twice before in the modern history of major hockey has one team so dominated the sport. The Ottawa Senators in 1920 and 1921 won both championships. The Montreal Canadiens repeated the feat in

RANGERS

0

RED WINGS

3

Detroit,
April 15, 1937

1930 and 1931.

The Red Wings are the first American team to win both of hockey's major championships twice in succession.

In beating the Rangers, Detroit conquered the league's sensation. Taking third place in the American section of the league, just qualifying for a playoff position, the Rangers defeated the Toronto Maple Leafs in two straight games and duplicated the performance against the Montreal Maroons to qualify for the Finals with the Red Wings. In those four games, only one goal was scored on Dave Kerr, the Rangers' goalie.

The Rangers continued their pace in the first game with the Red Wings. They won, 5-1, in Madison Square Garden. Then the series was transferred to Detroit and the Wings squared the series with a 4-2 victory. But in the third game the Rangers, retaliated with a 1-0 victory, beating the Red Wings on the Olympia ice for the first time in two years. The Wings, with everything at stake in

the fourth game, played sensationally and shut out the Rangers. Marty Barry scored Detroit's lone goal.

Tied at two victories each, everything was at stake in Thursday night's game. And it was the best game of the playoffs. Both teams were at their peak. Both were skating fast and checking hard.

The Rangers played well. The Red Wings, with Ebbie Goodfellow available only in the first period, played magnificently.

Marty Barry, whose big-money shot won the fourth game and kept the Red Wings in the series, scored two goals, one in the first period and another in the third. Johnny Sorrell, whose best hockey was reserved for the playoffs against the Rangers, got Detroit's other goal in the second period.

But it was the superb play of Earl Robertson, the man considered not good enough for major league hockey, that dominated the game.

Robertson, filling in for Normie Smith, the leading goaltender of the season, was good in his first two games with the team, great in the game the Wings won, 1-0, and magnificent Thursday night. The Olympia Stadium thought Hec Kilrea might join him. Kilrea slid into the boards headfirst with a thud that was felt in every corner of Olympia. But the veteran who disdains head gear, just shook his head gingerly and resumed play.

Disallowal of the Rangers' goal in the second period fooled Referee Stewart as completely as anyone in Olympia. When the red light flashed, Stewart skated to the press box and announced "Pratt from Neil Colville and Shibicky." Not for several seconds did Stewart notice the heated conference that followed Referee Mickey Ion's nullification of the tally.

Johnny Sorrell did not see his goal go into the net. He was spilled just as he shot but from his prone position. Sorrell looked up and saw the red light on. The sight caused him to lie back and kick his feet with sheer joy.

Midway in the game, Stewart skated over to Louis Giffels, the Olympia general manager, and demanded that a spectator along the boards be removed for his abusive language. The spectator was not ejected but was quietly removed to another section of the arena where he would be out of earshot of the referee.

Methodical Johnny Gallagher refuses to let winning the Stanley Cup interrupt his after-game routine. With near hysteria prevailing in the dressing room, Gallagher calmly plowed through the mass of visitors to the scales. He had lost six pounds

Red Wings owner James Norris (left) and Jack Adams celebrate the team's Stanley Cup win.

— no more, no less that usual.

Beer, under the Adams ban during the season, appeared almost the second players reached the dressing room.

Distinctions of rank and file were unrecognized after the game. A photographer, attempting to get a picture of a cluster of Wings, asked an elderly man in civilian clothes to step out of range. The request was unheard, so Boze Bordeau, the Pittsburgh trainer, to further photographic recognition of the heroes, firmly moved the gentle-

man out of the way. He happened to be James Norris, owner of the Wings.

Tommy Bridges left the Henry Ford Hospital long enough to cheer the Wings to victory.

Before the game the Stanley Cup was brought into the Detroit dressing room. Jack Adams used it as Exhibit A in his farewell address to the Wings.

"Every one of us from the time we were kids, shooting pucks on icy sidewalks, wanted to get his name on that Cup," said Adams.

WINGS KEEP BLACKHAWKS' CHAMPAGNE ON ICE

5-1 Victory Keeps Faint Playoff Hopes Alive

By Mark Beltaire

The Detroit News

Victory over the Chicago Blackhawks on Olympia ice Sunday night gave the Red Wings at least a 48-hour reprieve from oblivion. Jack Adams' motion for a full pardon has still to be acted upon by three clubs — the Canadiens at Montreal Tuesday, the Maple Leafs Thursday and the Rangers on Sunday.

BLACKHAWKS

1

RED WINGS

5

Detroit,
April 15, 1938

If any one of them refuses to acquiesce in the plea that Detroit deserves a place in the Stanley Cup playoffs, the Wings will be left on the sidelines while six other teams scramble for the championship trophy.

The burden of proof rest on the Wings. The situation was well expressed by Bill Stewart, manager of the Hawks, who said after his club had been forced by a 5-1 vote to grant Detroit a temporary stay of sentence.

Carl Liscombe

"We still hold a lead of four points. The Wings must get five out of six points in their three remaining games to beat us out. If they lose one, they're through. If we win one of the two we have left with the Americans and Boston, we're in no matter what they do."

Whatever the final verdict may be — and there seems little doubt that the decision will go against Detroit — the Wings can recall with pride their performance in a court where goals replace words as arguments

and sticks are the gavels used to bring recalcitrant "lawyers" to order.

Carl Liscombe, the young left winger from Gait, Ont., was far and away the most persuasive attorney for the defense. He spent 16 minutes preparing his brief, and then within the next 112 seconds, fired three such convincing arguments at Mike Karakas that the Chicago goalie was completely baffled, and the reprieve won.

Liscombe not only saved the Wings temporarily with his "hat trick," but also wiped out the former record for rapid-fire goals by the wide margin of 4 minutes 38 seconds. Nels Stewart, the Americans' center, set the old mark last New Year's Eve when he drove in three goals against the Maroons in 6 ½ minutes.

Lewis, who performed the "hat trick" himself only a week ago, was the first teammate to congratulate the joyful rookie while the crowd of 10,031 spectators bellowed its approval.

"Boy, I sure needed them," he grinned afterwards. "I'd set 20 points as my goal this year. I thought I'd never make it, but now I'm only one away."

RED WINGS WIN THIRD STANLEY CUP

Mowers Blanks Bruins to Sweep Series

By John Walter

Special to The Detroit News

Hilariously happy but tired and glad it's all over with, the Red Wings were en route to Detroit today, bearing the Stanley Cup as token of their capture of the world's hockey championship for the third time in Detroit's 17 years in the National Hockey League.

One of the greatest feats of net-minding in the game, 120 minutes of blocking the goal mouth in Stanley Cup play, earned Johnnie Mowers the plaudits of friend and foe alike as he gained his second shutout over the Bruins, 2-0, Thursday night to end the series in four straight games. Just 24 hours earlier he shut them out, 4-0. Curly-headed Joe Carveth and Chunky Carl Liscombe netted the goals, unassisted, that brought Detroit final victory. It squared the four straight defeats the Bruins handed the Wings in the Cup Finals two years ago and blotted memory of last year's heartbreaking

RED WINGS

2

———

BRUINS

0

Boston,
April 8, 1943

defeat at the hands of Toronto.

The goal paid off double for Liscombe, for he equaled the Stanley Cup scoring record of 14 points with six goals and eight assists. But even his feat was overshadowed by the performances of Mowers, the 28-year-old Niagara Falls, Ont., product.

"There's no doubt who won that game — Mowers did," was the tribute of Joe Carveth, who started the Wings on their way to victory. Even the most partisan of the 12,954 spectators who howled for the Wings' scalps as the desperate Bruins put up their greatest fight of the series, acknowledged Mowers' great performance.

Just how hard the Bruins fought is shown by the stops. Thirty times Mowers had to turn back Bruin shots. One he stopped with his head, in a tumultuous third period, which saw the Wings two men short at one point. Blood poured from a gash under his eye. Mowers refused to delay the game to be sewed up. He

tended the goal the last five minutes with blood streaming down his face and it wasn't until the train was pulling out of Boston's South Station, with the last of the breathless Wings just piling aboard, that Dr. C.I. Tomsu took two stitches in it.

From the moment play began it was obvious it was going to be a rough game, as 16 penalties subsequently proved. In the first three minutes, Eddie Wares was boarded and suffered what might be a broken wrist.

Nine minutes of the first period passed before the first fighting occurred. Carveth brawled with Ben Guidolin at the boards as Carveth tried to clear the puck. At the same moment, Jimmy Orlando, constantly booed by the fans throughout two games here, was high-sticked by Don Gallinger and retaliated.

All four were sent off the ice by referee Bill Chadwick. A minute after he came back on, Carveth broke away for the Wings' first goal in one of the finest plays executed by a Wing all year. Orlando poke-checked the puck to center ice and Boston's masterful Bill Cowley wheeled, raced

The 1942-43 Red Wings won both the regular-season championship and the Stanley Cup.

But the 24-year-old Regina, Sask., youth who overcame two broken legs to become a Red Wing regular, drove after Cowley with the fury of a mad man. Before Cowley could swing the puck out of Carveth's reach, the black-haired youngster overtook him. As they shot over Boston's blue line, Carveth was even. His legs on his stick and shouldered past Boston's ace just in time to break in the clear and make one feint with the puck before he drove it between Brimsek's legs.

Once later that period Detroit had a two-man advantage over the Bruins but failed to realize. It was shortly after the offending Bruins were back on, early in the second period, that Liscombe racked his goal.

Liscombe carried the puck almost the length of the ice, artfully evading defenseman Jack Crawford, one of the Bruins stalwarts in this series. Liscombe, who possesses the hardest shot of any left-winger in hockey today, whistled the puck over Brimsek's left shoulder. It hit a rear post and bounced out as the light flashed.

Crawford couldn't believe the puck had gone in, delayed play while he skated back to question the goal judge.

The climax came when Cowley got the puck 10 feet in front of the net with Mowers sprawled out of reach of the puck and Abel also ran out of reach.

"There was a big grin on Cowley's face," Abel related afterwards. "He nursed it along a few inches and then flicked it." But Cowley missed the corner of the net. The puck rolled away. It was the Bruins' last chance.

RED WINGS BREAK EIGHT RECORDS IN 15-0 WIN

Howe's Hat Trick Paces Rout of Rangers

By John Walter

The Detroit News

Because it was the greatest scoring debacle in the 28 years' history of the National Hockey League, fans will remember the astounding feats the Detroit Red Wings achieved when they routed New York Rangers, 15-0, at Olympia Sunday night. It will take nearly a page to cover the eight scoring marks they established in the official record books.

The Wings, by virtue of their victory, replaced Boston in third place in the NHL standings; Syd Howe became the Wings' top scorer for all-time with 149 goals through his feat of turning the "hat trick" in Sunday's third period; three others, Murray Armstrong, Don Grosso and Joe Carveth, also each counted five scoring points in the night's play.

The victory marked the Wings' seventh straight without defeat, their fourth consecutive win; Conrad Dion, the "Asbestos Kid," has a

RANGERS

0

RED WINGS

15

Detroit,
Jan. 23, 1944

record of five games without a defeat and a record of allowing the opposition an average of only two goals a game.

The Wings can climb within a point of second-place Toronto by winning at Boston Tuesday night. The Wings boast a potentially wide margin over the Leafs, having played four less games than Toronto.

It will be a long time before some of Sunday night's records are erased — and there were 12,293 witnesses.

Eleven of the Wings' 13 men in uniform figured in the scoring. Cully Simon, the Wing defenseman, was the only one, outside of Goalie Dion, who didn't get a point. Ten of the remaining 11 counted one or more goals. Joe Carveth, the lone exception, was too busy setting 'em up for the others, his five assists being high for the night, just one short of the NHL record set by Montreal's Elmer Lach last year.

The game didn't start out like a

rout. The Rangers' Bryan Hextall fired at the Wings' net in the first minute. Referee Norman Lamport overruled New York's goal claim only after conferring with goal judge John Miller. Less than two minutes later, Armstrong flipped in Harold Jackson's rebound for the Wings' goal. Bill Quackenbush counted the Wings' second goal at the tail end of the period with the Wings shorthanded.

Here's how: Howe, Bruneteau, Quackenbush and Hollett had such mastery of the puck when Simon was sent to the penalty box, they passed it back and forth 90 seconds without the five Rangers on the ice — Hextall, Hiller, Aubuchon and the two McDonalds, Jack and Bucko, once touching the puck. When Hextall finally got it. Hollett spun him around with a check, put Quackenbush in the clear with a quick pass, and the latter scored on a 10-footer with Hiller hanging on his shoulders.

Bob Dill, the Rangers' rookie defenseman, helped precipitate the slaughter that followed when he was twice penalized in less than four minutes with the second period eight minutes old. In a space of six minutes, the Wings counted four goals:

n Liscombe scored on a 30-footer.

n Bruneteau counted unassisted, while Dill was off.

n In between Dill's penalties, Brown scored.

n Dill had just returned when Jackson flashed the light with a 65-footer along the ice.

Before the period ended, Kenny Kilrea counted his first goal since leaving the Army to make it 7-0.

Then came the third period and eight goals.

Kilrea hit the post twice as the Wings ganged up in New York's end of the ice.

Liscombe led with a 20-footer, first of six goals in 10 minutes. Grosso counted two, Howe one, then Hollett and Armstrong.

After Grosso made his pair, the Wings were so frantic for points, the Rangers' center, Johnny Mahaffy, got a clean break-away. He didn't fool Dion.

With the game waning, Howe came through with two goals 18 seconds apart to become the Wings' all-time scoring leader.

As the fans shouted themselves hoarse, urging on the Wings in this bizarre scoring spectacle, three Wings broke away without a Ranger between them and the hapless McAuley. They passed the puck buck and forth to bewilder

Syd Howe's "hat trick" in the third period made him the Wings' all-time scorer with 149 goals.

McAuley — and to give each other an assist point. As they got to the goal mouth and green light flashed, ending the game. The puck went in the net and three Red Wings skated off the ice, frustrated because their dallying had robbed them of a scoring point apiece.

HOWE SCORES 6 GOALS IN WIN OVER RANGERS

New Single-Game Scoring Record Established

By John Walter

The Detroit News

Modern hockey's greatest individual scoring feat — six goals in a single game — was the achievement Thursday night at Olympia of Sydney Harris Howe, center, now in his 15th pro season, his 10th with the Red Wings.

RANGERS
2

RED WINGS
12

Detroit,
Feb. 3, 1944

Syd Howe's "double hat trick" against the New York Rangers was the first ever in National Hockey League history.

The 32-year-old Howe counted two goals in each period as the Red Wings overwhelmed the New York Rangers, 12-2. The victory was the Wings' ninth in 11 starts. In 28 days they have climbed from fifth to second place. They now are two points ahead of Toronto, whom they engage in a doubleheader this weekend; there Saturday, here Sunday.

A machinist at Ford by day and a hockey player at night, Howe is the first to turn a "double hat trick" in NHL history. Thus he forces into oblivion the records of such hockey greats as Howie Morenz, Joe Malone, Babe Dye, Charlie Conacher, Pit Lepine and Harry Broadbent, all of whom made five goals in a game.

Sharing honors with Howe was Don Grosso. Grosso equaled two NHL individual scoring records, one for six assists and another for seven scoring points, since he collected one goal himself. Grosso assisted on five of Howe's goals. Grosso claimed he should have had an assist on all of Howe's goals, which should have given him two NHL marks. On a goal in question, when Cully Simon got

Howe scored his goals in pairs had the 8,147 paid customers and 900 patrol boys in a frenzy early in the third period which was when Howe's chance of setting a record better apparent.

Howe's brace of goals in the first period were 18 seconds apart. Grosso set Howe up in front of the net and Howe outgolfed Bucko McDonald for his first goal at 11:27.

Howe clicked his second goal on Harold Jackson's rebound at 11:45 to make the score, 3-0. Liscombe having scored earlier.

The second period was nearly over when Howe connected for No. 3. Simon threw the puck to him from behind the net and he whipped a 25-footer in the far corner that Goalie Ken McAuley didn't have a chance on.

Sixty-two seconds later, Howe stole the puck from Dutch Hiller, got a return pass from Grosso and raced in to beat McAuley. Howe took a nose dive to the ice as McAuley came out to block him. That made four consecutive goals for Howe since the Wings' other score at the close of the second period came on Simon's 40-footer that bounced in off Bruneteau's foot.

The crowd groaned as Howe shot the puck over the net early in the third period, but half a minute later, Mud Bruneteau and Grosso set him up again. Howe feinted McAuley. As the latter lunged to the right, Howe flicked the puck right over McAuley into the net.

"That was the classic goal of the

Jack Adams (center) celebrates the Wings' win over New York with Harry Lumley (left) and Ed Bruneteau.

night," Jack Adams said afterward. Howe was given a tremendous ovation as the announcement came over the loud speaker that the all-time NHL record had been equaled.

Only 57 seconds later, Howe brought the wildly cheering spectators to their feet again with goal No. 6. Bruneteau started the play, passing to Grosso who carried the puck within 10 feet of the goalmouth. Only Hiller remained in front of the Ranger goalie and Hiller jabbed at the puck as Grosso attempted to pass it back to Howe. For a moment, the puck was at their feet, then Howe had it, flicking it in to beat McAuley easily.

Howe was given a tremendous ovation as he skated off the ice. From then

on, both sides played streamlined hockey, racing at each other's goal with virtually no body-checking. One exception was when Jackson elected to hit Bucko McDonald at mid-ice. Bucko ducked, got through to score the Rangers' first goal in nearly 170 minutes of play with the Wings. Grosso, Flash Hollett and Liscombe scored in the remaining minutes and so did the Rangers' Fernand Gauthier.

Bruneteau's goal brought his season's total to 26, exceeding Ebbie Goodfellow's 1931 record. Goodfellow was among the first to congratulate Bruneteau and Howe after the Wings, led by Capt. Flash Hollett, carried the grinning Howe on their shoulders to the dressing room.

RED WINGS STOP MAPLE LEAFS AGAIN

Detroit Scores 5 Goals in 1:39

Special to The Detroit News

Coach Jack Adams of the Detroit Red Wings seems to have hit upon the formula for victory over the Toronto Maple Leafs in the National Hockey League. The Wings defeated the Leafs, 8-4, last night for the second time this season, each team doubling its score over their meeting in Detroit on Sunday night, when Adams' team had a 4-2 margin.

RED WINGS
8

MAPLE LEAFS
4

Toronto,
Nov. 15, 1944

Before meeting the Red Wings, the Leafs had bowled over the Montreal Canadiens twice, New York Rangers twice, Boston Bruins once and the Chicago Blackhawks once for six straight victories and the league leadership. They still hold the leadership after their two losses to Detroit but now they only have a two-point margin over Montreal, which in turn leads the third-place Wings by two points.

Jack Adams' brilliant coaching made the difference in the Red Wings' win over Toronto.

Adams' victory recipe seems to consist of tying up the Bodnar-Schriner-Carr line which carried the Leafs to their previous six triumphs. They failed to get a scoring point Sunday night in Detroit and they were muzzled again last night by consistent back-checking on the part of Syd Howe and Modere (Mud) Bruneteau and by some near-mirac-

ulous saves by Connie Dion in the Red Wings' goal.

Bill (Flash) Hollett was the spark-plug of the Detroit attack last night. The big defenseman scored two unassisted goals, and his defensive play was of a high order. Rookie Steve Wochy was the top Detroit point-getter, however, with one goal and two assists. Other goals were tallied by Bruneteau, Jud McAtee, Carl Liscombe, Harold Jackson and Don Grosso. Howe, Murray Armstrong and Grosso had an assist each.

Ted (Teeter) Kennedy, the 18-year-old native of Port Colborne, Ont., was the chief Toronto offensive threat. He scored two goals in 20 seconds of the third period and assisted on another by Bob Davidson. Bill Ezinicki collected three assists. Nick Metz got the other Toronto goal, assisted by Mel Hill.

Eight of the 12 goals were scored in the third period, five for Detroit and three for Toronto. Three of the Detroit goals — by Jackson, Wochy and Grosso — came in 28 seconds while defenseman Reg Hamilton of Toronto served a tripping penalty.

ALL WINGS NEED – TIE OR VICTORY OVER RANGERS

Final Playoff Spot Almost Locked Up

By Paul Chandler

The Detroit News

Olympia has the hockey playoff tickets filed neatly in the box office, and why not?

Detroit today is five points in front of New York and strategically set to finish the season in fourth place, the last play-off spot.

Olympia's management ordered the tickets last week when the situation was far left favorable, but results of the weekend would indicate there is a prophet in the box office.

There is only one slim way in which the crisp new tickets now could become worthless pasteboard. If Detroit should lose both of its remaining games and the Rangers sweep their last three, the Red Wings would be nipped by a single point.

All doubt could be eliminated here Wednesday. On that night the Rangers meet the Red Wings for

RANGERS
6
———
RED WINGS
10

Detroit,
March 16, 1947

the last time. If Detroit wins or gets a tie, the playoff issue automatically is closed.

Until the matter is settled, of course, no playoff dates will be announced, and no tickets sold.

Detroit raced to a 10-6 triumph at Chicago Sunday night while the Rangers lost to Montreal, 4-3 in New York.

This followed the previous night's results, in which Detroit humbled the Blackhawks here, and New York lost a heartbreaking 1-0 decision in Montreal. The results of these two evenings of play increased Detroit's lead over New York from a scant one point to a fat five.

Detroit made the Blackhawks look ridiculous on both Saturday and Sunday.

The Saturday game ended 8-3, but the Red Wings had a 6-0 lead before they eased up. On Sunday the Wings were out in front, 8-2, before cutting the throttle.

Certain of the Red Wings indulged in a gluttonous scoring feast. Ray Conacher whipped four goals past Emil Francis Sunday night to run his season total to 29, which makes him second man in the league in that department.

Ted Lindsay, the man whom Jack Adams calls "the best left wing in the league," scored five goals in two nights, two on Saturday and three on Sunday.

Billy Taylor acquired 10 points in the series: A goal and two assists Saturday and seven assists Sunday.

Now he has 61 points for the season and stands third among the individual scoring, trailing only Maurice Richard and Max Bentley.

In their remaining three games, the Rangers can almost depend on one victory.

They close with this same Chicago club in New York next Sunday. In addition to the game here Wednesday, they also play at Toronto Saturday.

Detroit has only the Ranger game and a finale with the Leafs

When Hockeytown Was Known as Cup Town

Red Wings Won Four Titles in Six Seasons in the 1950's

By Vartan Kupelian
The Detroit News

T he time and place are etched in the annals of the Detroit Red Wings.

The story has been told and re-told so often it has reached epic proportions.

There are countless watershed occasions in the history of the Red Wings but few can match what happened on April 15, 1952, at venerable Olympia Stadium on Detroit's west side.

It's the stuff of legends.

For those who have followed the history of the Red Wings, the date isn't obscure. It marks the deciding game of the 1952 Stanley Cup playoffs, won by the Red Wings.

It was in the spring of 1952 that the Wings achieved something no other club ever had. They won the Stanley Cup in eight straight playoff games, sweeping first the Toronto Maple Leafs and then the Montreal Canadiens.

There have never been two more daunting opponents. Yet the Wings dominated because goaltender Ter- ry Sawchuk and a tidy, diligent defense strangled the big guns of the Maple Leafs and Canadiens. Of the eight playoff games, the Wings won four by shutout.

Something else happened, too. Somebody threw an octopus onto the ice to celebrate the Stanley Cup triumph. It flew out of Section 10 at Olympia Stadium at about the midway point of the deciding game against Montreal.

This next little bit of information is the stuff of classic trivia. The crea- ture's legs measured 14 inches. Some say The Original Octopus was alive; some say it was dead.

Bob Goldham, the rugged Detroit defenseman, flipped it over on the blade of his hockey stick, and an usher retrieved it, not to the penalty bin but to the press box for fur-

Terry Sawchuk, who replaced Harry Lumley as the Red Wings' goalie, became a legend at shutting out opponents.

ther inspection by the media.

Upon discussion, one of the writers suggested The Original Octopus should make an appearance on television between periods. The idea was dismissed out of hand. What was the purpose of the cameo appearance by the eight-legged creature? Was it a joke or was there significance attached to it?

It is widely accepted that the eight legs of the octopus represented the eight victories of the Wings' playoff sweep.

However, at the time, there were other theories. Was it a random act of a prankster or a well-conceived plot? It was pointed out that octopus is derived from Greek — oktopous, okto for eight and pous for foot.

There is also a ancient dictionary definition of the word on point: "An organization with many branches through which it maintains a hold on others."

After all, the Red Wings — in the glory years of the early 1950's — maintained a hold on others. They were the scourge of the National Hockey League, winning seven straight regular-season league titles and four Stanley Cup championships.

Before Detroit became Hockeytown, as it has been known in the 1990's, it was Cup Town. Today, the arrival of the octopus is a playoff rite

and among the most enduring traditions in professional sports — and certainly in Detroit sports.

For 40 years, the Red Wings were the model of a highly efficient and successful sports franchise. They captured seven Stanley Cup championships, the most for a United States-based National Hockey

The Detroit News
Pictorial
MAGAZINE
Presidential Playground
See Page 5
December 4   1949

Lindsay, Abel and Howe, the Red Wings "front line"

League team. Many of the greatest names and personalities in league history have worn Detroit's distinctive winged-wheel crest, from Marty Barry, Larry Aurie and Ebbie Goodfellow in the early days, to Sid Abel, Terry Sawchuk and Gordie Howe in the glory years.

Detroit was awarded an NHL franchise for the 1926-27 season, a fact which belies its popularly held designation as one of the league's Original Six. In reality, the Wings were an expansion team. They joined the NHL a decade after its formation during an era that often has been described the Golden Age of Sports.

In 1927, the world of sports already had Babe Ruth, Red Grange, Bobby Jones, Jack Dempsey and Bill Tilden and now hockey, a Canadian game, was invading America. New York was adding a second team in 1926-27, the Rangers, to join the existing New York Americans. The success of the Americans, playing a Canadian game before audiences in the Big Apple, spawned expansion in the United States.

The other new franchises in the United States were Detroit and Chicago.

The Detroit team was known as the Cougars. The team's nickname was later changed to the "Falcons" and, finally, the "Red Wings" when the club was purchased by industrialist James (Pop) Norris in 1932.

With the Cougars franchise in place, the critical building block toward the ultimate goal of a championship was put in place a year lat-

(Left to right) Gordie Howe, Marcel Bonin, Glen Skov, Johnny Wilson and Marty Pavelich led the Red Wings to the Stanley Cup in 1954-55.

(Jack) Adams as coach. He would become more than just a coach. He would become the architect of one of the most successful teams in sports history.

Another of the indispensable elements of the Wings' history is the genesis of the winged-wheel logo. There's never been a sports emblem which combines the immediate recognition factor with such understated elegance. In that respect, it is the best logo in sports. It defines not only a team but a city.

The logo was the brainchild of Pop Norris, who had played in the Montreal Athletic Association for a team named the Winged Wheelers. The team's symbol was a golden winged wheel, but the wings were vertical and the wheel was a gristmill, which is used for grinding grain. Norris altered the design slightly, turning the wing sideways.

The winged-wheel is one of the few things Jack Adams didn't have to alter upon his arrival in Detroit for the 1927-28 season. He promptly went to work on building a winning foundation that would remain intact throughout his 35 years with the hockey club.

Adams, from western Canada, was a star forward for teams in Toronto and Ottawa before becoming Detroit's general manager and coach. There was never any question who ran the show with Adams around. He could be crusty or jolly, sometimes both at once, but he was always in control.

Adams kept each player's salary figures on index cards that he carried in the breast pocket of his suit coat. He would negotiate contracts by writing a figure on the card. With only six NHL teams in those days and plenty of players trying to break

into the big leagues, players had little choice but to accept his offers. If they resisted, they were gone. It was Adams' way, or the highway.

Nobody knew the game better than Adams, and that knowledge was essential in moving the club up through the standings in a very short time. By the mid-1930's, the Red Wings were the league power, winning Stanley Cup titles in 1936 and 1937.

The 1936 playoffs produced one of the sport's most memorable moments.

The opening game between the Red Wings and the Montreal Maroons was scoreless through three periods and five overtime periods. With 3½ minutes left in the sixth extra period, Mud Bruneteau finally scored against Montreal goalie Lorne Chabot. Detroit goaltender Normie Smith didn't allow a goal in the longest game ever played — 176 minutes and 30 seconds.

The Wings went on to quickly dispatch the Canadiens, winning the series three games to zero.

The Wings were the dominant team again in 1937. Four Detroit players — right wing Larry Aurie, center Marty Barry, defenseman Ebbie Goodfellow and goalie Smith

During Jack Adams' tenure, the Red Wings won the Stanley Cup in 1936, 1937, 1943, 1950, 1952, 1954 and 1955.

— were named to the six-man All-Star team. They had enough firepower to defeat the New York Rangers three games to two in the five-game final series for the Stanley Cup.

Adams' team won a third Stanley Cup in 1943, sweeping the Boston Bruins in four games, but the Red Wings at that time were just revving up for some truly great years.

The Glory Years — 1949 to 1955 — were on the horizon.

The Detroit team assembled by Adams in the late 1940's and early 1950's was one of the great dynasties in the history of sports. Beginning with the 1948-49 season, the Red Wings won a league-record seven straight NHL regular-season championships and four Stanley Cup titles.

The team had many strengths and few weaknesses. The famed Production Line (a reference to Detroit's automotive history) consisted of the stately Sid Abel centering Gordie Howe, then only 21, and Ted Lindsay. Abel and Lindsay were tremendous players in their own right and the three future members of the Hall of Fame formed a lethal offensive machine for Tommy Ivan, who had taken over as coach of the Red Wings when Adams moved himself upstairs to concentrate on management duties.

"They could score goals in their sleep," Adams said.

Lindsay, Abel and Howe finished 1-2-3 in the league scoring race in

the 1949-50 season en route to the first of four Stanley Cups. But the winning goal in the seventh game of the Finals against the New York Rangers came from an unlikely source.

Peter Joseph Babando, a stubborn hockey player, wouldn't be denied by his stable of more skillful teammates.

It was at 12:11 a.m., April 24, 1950, that Babando made the shot heard 'round the NHL. It gave Detroit a 4-3 victory over the Rangers — and the Stanley Cup.

In Game 7, the Wings rallied from a two-goal deficit to force overtime on goals by Babando and Abel just 21 seconds apart. Comebacks were nothing new to the Red Wings that year. Facing elimination, they won two straight against Toronto and did the same against the Rangers. Detroit had several great scoring chances, with Babando's goal a fitting climax to this dramatic series.

Abel, the Wings' captain, embraced the silver chalice. Adams and owner Jim Norris joined in the ceremony but the crowd wanted more. The Olympia throng of 13,095 — on its feet — chanted, "We want Howe! We want Howe!"

In civilian clothes, Howe strolled to center ice to join his teammates. It was during the 1949-50 playoffs that Howe, the game's budding superstar, suffered a near-fatal head injury.

What made the incident so

alarming is that Howe's physical presence had reached mythical proportions. His teammates called him "Power." He was 6 feet tall and 200 pounds, with shoulders that sloped from a thick neck. He had a mean streak which made him a fearsome figure. He could lift opponents with one arm or brush them aside with a flick of a wrist. If he felt an opponent had trespassed too far into his personal territory or taken advantage of a teammate, Howe doled out retribution discreetly and swiftly. Soon, opposing players learned to avoid Howe and his domain.

Yet, he had to overcome several injuries early in his career, the most serious of which came in 1950 when he was slammed into the boards by Toronto's Ted Kennedy. The head injury suffered by Howe required surgery and jeopardized not only his playing career but his life.

So when the Wings moved on to the Stanley Cup Finals against the Rangers after dispatching Toronto, they were without Howe. In the end, the injury became just one more obstacle the greatest player in history had to overcome to reach his destiny.

That was the setting when Howe, his hair still closely-cropped, visited with his teammates in the victorious locker room after Babando's goal had given Detroit the Cup.

"You big, lucky stiff," Lindsay said to his linemate over the din of the dressing room. "You sit in the seats

and watch us go out and make a couple thousand dollars for you!"

There was an interesting post-series controversy. The Rangers accused the Wings of taking Benzedrine cocktails to enhance their performance.

Nonsense, the Wings said.

Coach Tommy Ivan laughed off the suggestion, adding, "Sugar cubes dipped in brandy? Yes, they've had it a number of times. Sugar is recognized as the quickest energy builder there is and a few drops of brandy helps its action. Remember, we tried oxygen tanks in the Toronto playoffs last year but Benzedrine? Never!"

The Red Wings reached the Finals in the 1949-50 season by

ousting three-time defending champion Toronto in a major upset. The seven-game series was decided by Leo Reise's overtime goal, a long backhander which beat Toronto goalie Turk Broda, for a 1-0 triumph. It was the series in which Howe was hospitalized and produced a vicious blood-letting.

Once past the initial repercussions, the Detroit-Toronto match-up was taut and tough, the kind of game which later popularized the notion of "old-time hockey."

Howe was injured in the opener, a 5-0 Toronto victory, and Game 2 quickly got out of hand. There were two bench-clearing brawls. The antagonistic Lindsay, as would be expected, was right in the middle of the melee or, as a newspaper account of the game called it, "a general riot."

Every player threw and every player received punches. Kennedy, the man who was involved in the Howe collision and injury, speared Reise in the face, and Reise retaliated by dropping Toronto's Jimmy Thomson with a high-stick.

Lindsay went after Kennedy, and Toronto's Gus Mortson intervened on behalf of his teammate, only to be equalized by Abel.

It went on and on and didn't end until Reise's deciding goal.

For Adams, it was the sixth time his name was etched on the Stanley Cup. As a player, he helped the Toronto Arenas win the cup in 1918 and the Ottawa Senators in 1927. He managed the Wings to Cup victories in 1936, 1937 and 1943.

Adams, devoting himself entirely to managing duties, did a most unusual thing after the 1949-50 season. He broke up a winning combination with a big trade which sent Cup-winning goaltender Harry Lumley to Chicago in a nine-player deal that shook the NHL.

Also going to the Blackhawks were Stanley Cup hero Pete Babando, Al Dewsbury and Don Morrison, forwards; and defenseman Jack Stewart, a First-Team All-Star three times. The Wings received defenseman Bob Goldham, forwards Gaye Stewart and Metro Prystrai and goalie Jim Henry.

But Adams, the wily manager, had no intention of turning the netminding duties over to Henry. The trade was a calculated moved aimed at giving a young goaltender named Terry Sawchuk, 20, a chance to play in the big leagues.

The results were spectacular. Sawchuk posted a league-leading 11 shutouts as a rookie.

The Red Wings won the regular season, only to be eliminated in the playoffs by Montreal.

The Canadiens won the first two games on overtime goals by Maurice (The Rocket) Richard. The Wings rebounded with two straight victories before Montreal reasserted itself to end the series in six games. Ironically, the Wings, the scourge of the regular season, had finished with 36 points more than the Canadiens.

But Adams' move would pay long-term dividends. Sawchuk's play in goal enabled the Red Wings to win the Stanley Cup in three of the next four seasons.

The Red Wings experienced one of the greatest seasons ever in 1951-52.

Howe won his second consecutive scoring title with 49 goals and 87 points. Linemate Lindsay also made the All-Star team, as did Sawchuk and defenseman Red Kelly. Sawchuk won the Vezina Trophy with a 1.94 goals-against average and 12 shutouts. The Wings won a fourth straight regular season championship. For the second year in a row, they chalked up 100 points or

more and finished 22 points ahead of runner-up Montreal.

In the playoffs, the Red Wings didn't lose a single game. Sawchuk allowed only five goals and posted four shutouts in the eight playoff games, a truly remarkable feat. Sawchuk's playoff goals-against average was 0.62.

The Wings' dominance did not surprise Adams, the architect. "This is a fine team that has won everything else and the guys intend to enter the record books as the first club to do the job in eight," Adams had said.

Joe Primeau, the Toronto coach, marveled at the Wings' majesty. "They're a wonderfully balanced team," Primeau said. "They just keep comin' and comin' at you, and if you do get through, down there at the end of the rink is that Sawchuk."

That Sawchuk, indeed!

The Canadiens made it into the Finals, thanks to Rocket Richard's goal-scoring exploits, but the Habs had no chance against the Detroit juggernaut. There would be no repeat of the upset from the year before. The Red Wings were too good, too determined and too angry.

They wanted vengeance and they got it.

The Red Wings won four straight games, with Sawchuk posting his third and fourth shutouts, and Howe and Lindsay combining for five goals to spearhead the offense.

The great Production Line was

broken up before the 1952-53 season when Adams traded Abel to Chicago, where the veteran center embarked on the next stage of his long, distinguished NHL career as a player-coach.

Of course, Adams had someone waiting in the wings to replace Abel as center on the big line. That's how Adams operated. One of the tenets of his managing philosophy was always to make room for younger players by dealing older players.

Of course, the key was to know exactly when the right time was and Adams was uncanny. He knew the right time to deal Harry Lumley. He knew the right time to deal Sid Abel.

Just as Sawchuk, the brilliant young goalie, was poised to step in for Lumley, Adams had a bright young center waiting in the wings. Alex Delvecchio, a slick playmaker, was a perfect fit between Howe and Lindsay. Both wingers could score with the best in the NHL and Delvecchio was adept as making a play, a pass or scoring himself. Delvecchio had 43 assists that first year, plus 16 goals.

If it's possible, the Production Line was even better, even more productive, and the Wings romped to another regular season title, their fifth straight. In the process, Howe became the first player in NHL history to win the scoring title three straight seasons. He had 49 goals and 95 points and both he and Lindsay made the First All-Star team for the third straight year.

But the Red Wings stumbled in the playoffs against an outmanned Boston squad, thanks to the Bruins goalie, Sugar Jim Henry — the same man the Wings had acquired, then traded away, in favor of Sawchuk.

"I would compare this year's Wing squad with some of the best I've handled in my 26 years at Olympia, despite the playoffs," Adams said.

The dynasty might have been teetering at that point but it was far from over. Adams knew it, too. He could rant and rave with the best, but his reserved demeanor after the defeat indicated to those who followed hockey that there were more championships to come.

In the 1953-54 season, the Red Wings and Howe again ruled the NHL. Howe won a fourth straight scoring title with 81 points and the Wings ran their string of regular season crowns to a half-dozen. By now, Howe and Lindsay were fixtures on the All-Star First Team, and Red Kelly, the defenseman, was selected to the First Team for the third straight year. The All-Star goaltender was Toronto's Harry Lumley, the former Detroit star.

Kelly, a steady defenseman who played the position with an abundance of savvy and skill, became the first player to win a new award, the James Norris Trophy, as the NHL's best defenseman. The award was named in honor of the former owner of the Red Wings.

With so much firepower and defense, the Wings simply could not be denied a return engagement with the Stanley Cup. They eliminated Toronto in five games to set up another showdown with Montreal, the Canadiens having knocked out the Boston Bruins.

The new Production Line dominated early in the Finals as the Wings surged to a 3-1 series lead. The Canadiens made a crucial strategic decision, turning the goaltending duties over to Gerry McNeil, a call-up from the minors, instead of Jacques (Jake the Snake) Plante.

McNeil blanked the Red Wings in the fifth game, won on Ken Mosdell's overtime goal, and won again in Game 6.

Then came another of the great moments in Red Wings history.

Game 7 went into overtime with the Wings and Canadiens tied, 1-1. Less than five minutes into the extra session, with hockey's great prize at stake, Tony Leswick fired a shot at the Montreal goal and McNeil. Doug Harvey, the Canadiens' superstar defenseman, attempted to knock aside the airborne puck.

He wasn't quick enough to get a handle on the disk. It ricocheted off the defenseman's glove and flickered past the shoulder of the Montreal goaltender.

The Detroit Red Wings had won another Stanley Cup against an arch-rival.

In 1956, the Red Wings played the Marquette Prison team — known as Emery's Boys.

There could be no sweeter outcome in hockey for the men in the winged-wheel jerseys.

By the 1954-55 season, the Montreal Canadiens were beginning to match the champion Red Wings in firepower and skill.

Les Habitants mightily wanted to take the Stanley Cup away from the American titleholder and the roster of the Province of Quebec's NHL entry looked every bit the part of a dragonslayer.

The cast included the elegant Jean Beliveau, the flamboyant Bernie (Boom Boom) Geoffrion, the terrific defenseman Doug Harvey and Jacques Plante in goal.

But the straw that stirred Montreal's drink remained Maurice (The Rocket) Richard, Howe's counterpart in the red, blue and white colors of the Canadiens.

Richard was a fiery Frenchman with a glare that could wither even the most stout-hearted opponent. He could score and scare. If Howe was the embodiment of the Red Wings, Richard was the heart and soul of the Canadiens.

They both played the same position, right wing, and played the same role — they were the go-to guys.

To no one's surprise, the Red Wings and Canadiens were locked in a tight battle for the regular-season title. If that wasn't enough, the famous riot on St. Catherine Street was about to put a charge into hockey.

Richard was on his way to the scoring title when, on March 13, 1955, in a game against the Bruins, he lost his composure. Richard's monumental temper had gotten him in trouble before but never to this extent. After a skirmish, he attacked the Bruins player, Hal Laycoe, with his stick, and when a linesman, Cliff Thompson, attempted to break it up, Richard took a punch at the official.

Clarence Campbell, the NHL president, was a man of steel and commitment.

He was outraged by Richard's behavior and, in the absence of a Players Association, he issued a ban that wouldn't be possible in today's sports climate.

Campbell banned Richard from the final three regular-season games and the playoffs. Four days later, Campbell attended a showdown game at the Forum in Montreal between the Canadiens and Red Wings.

His appearance was greeted by the partisan fans with howls and a barrage of thrown obstacles, followed by a tear gas cannister which landed on the ice. Campbell was not only verbally abused but also physically attacked by a Montreal fan.

It wasn't long before the trouble spilled outside the Forum. The fans poured out of the building onto St. Catherines and turned into a maddening crowd, a mob which looted stores and destroyed property on its march through the streets of Montreal, the city of churches.

It wasn't until Richard, himself, the next day pleaded for calm and a return to peace and civility did the riots ends. Richard said he would accept the punishment meted out by Campbell, with this proviso: He

would return the following season to lead the Canadiens to that holy land of Stanley Cup champions.

In the meantime, the Wings would go on to win a seventh straight regular-season title by a paltry two points over Montreal. In the playoff semifinals, the Wings ousted Toronto in four straight — sweeps were becoming a habit for the Detroit dynasty — and Montreal needed just five games to defeat Boston and set up the Finals showdown everybody was anticipating.

Detroit vs. Montreal. For all the marbles ... and the Stanley Cup.

The first six games were split with the home team prevailing in each, despite the fact the Canadiens did not have Richard. That set up a seventh game winner-take-all at Olympia Stadium, home of the Red Wings.

In the spring of 1955, Alex Delvecchio had reached the age of 23 and was an emerging young star in the NHL. Delvecchio had a reputation as a cool customer, no matter how heated the action.

Usually a sound sleeper, Delvecchio tossed and turned in bed the night before the Wings' seventh-game showdown against Montreal. "I lay awake thinking of the game coming up," Delvecchio said. "It's the first time it ever happened to me."

Perhaps Delvecchio knew something special was about to happen for him and his teammates. Delvec-

chio scored two goals and the great Gordie Howe another as the Red Wings defeated Montreal, 3-1, to win the Stanley Cup for the fourth time in seven years.

Delvecchio's goals were breathtaking. On the first, he cut across the goalmouth to send a 15-foot backhand shot past Montreal goaltender Jacques Plante as more than 15,000 Olympia Stadium fans cheered. Delvecchio's second goal came early in the third period on a solo effort to give Detroit an insurmountable three-goal margin.

"It's a great thrill," said the unflappable Delvecchio, whose performance under great pressure was about to elevate him to star status. "It's always nice to beat Montreal and it's best in the Stanley Cup playoffs."

Detroit and Montreal were the outstanding teams of that era, and any series matching them automatically had a place reserved in hockey history. But this Detroit team, according to the man who knew better than any other, was special.

"This is the greatest clutch team I've ever had," said Jack Adams, the general manager and architect of the glory years in Detroit hockey history. "They won every game that had to be won."

Along the way, they won more than just games. They captured the hearts of a city and its great and loyal hockey fans.

WINGS KNOW THEIR ABC'S (ADAMS, BABANDO, CUP)

Second Overtime Goal Gives Detroit its Fourth Title

By Paul Chandler

Special to The Detroit News

Into the New York nets blazed the golden goal at the exact moment of 12:11 a.m., April 24, 1950 — today.

Peter Joseph Babando, a stubborn hockey player whose personal comeback story will be noted later, made the shot and gave Detroit the game, 4-3.

Thousands of throats opened in Olympia to hail the shot, the goal, the game — and the new champions of the hockey empire, the Detroit Red Wings.

Hockey's grail, the silver Stanley Cup, thus came back to the United States, and to Detroit for the first time in seven years. It had been in Toronto or Montreal since being taken away from the Red Wings in 1943.

It comes to Detroit for the fourth time, the other years being 1943, 1937 and 1936.

In the view of 13,095 fans, weary, worn and aching Red Wings kissed and embraced, threw equipment to

RANGERS
3

RED WINGS
4

Detroit,
April 23, 1950

the ceiling, hoisted Coach Tommy Ivan to their shoulders, and went through all the stages of joyous emotion available to young athletes.

Tired players for the New York Rangers, the underdog team, said quick farewells and stepped off the stage, narrowly beaten after a dogged, honorable playoff stand.

President Clarence Campbell delivered the Cup as a "fitting climax to this dramatic series." Captain Sid Abel took it and hugged, his wet face twisted into a great grin.

Manager Jack Adams and Owner Jim Norris came to the middle of the rink and about that time the chant from the crowd gained the volume of thunder: "We want Howe! We want Howe!"

And, in civilian clothes, smiling Gordie Howe strolled to center ice to join his mates. Howe's hair was closely cropped, still growing out after a skull operation required by an injury early in the playoffs.

Photographers flashed handfuls

of bulbs. The stadium rang with organ music ... "the moon shines tonight on pretty Red Wing ..."

Players after many minutes trickled to their dressing room, mobbed at every step. They tossed their sticks to the crowd, the traditional sign of the last game of the season. Jack Stewart picked up a moppet and kissed her.

Once in the dressing room they roared, profanely and happily. Civilians streamed in to shake hands, pound backs and yell.

Ivan, a tired man, murmured, "They won it. The kids won it. Nobody could do it for them."

Lindsay hollered at Howe, "You big, lucky stiff. You sit in the seat and watch us go out and make a couple of thousand dollars for you!"

Finally, everybody was dressed, and Norris quietly told them all to come to a downtown hotel for the victory toast.

It was done in champagne, bottle after bottle popping open — some poured in the Stanley Cup — and slipped therefrom.

This, then, was the celebration of a long, hard hockey campaign

by a team that never failed to make a comeback.

To win the Cup, the Red Wings ploughed through 84 hockey games. Their last one, the game in Olympia Sunday night, was their longest. When it was over, they were more exhausted than ever before.

It didn't end until 8:31 of the second sudden death overtime, after midnight. It was the first time in history a playoff had gone down to the last game and then into extra periods before a decision could be reached.

Babando's goal settled the issue, and there's a special story about it ...

The score was 3-3. Detroit had wiped out a two-goal disadvantage to close out the regulation 60 minutes in a tie. Twenty minutes of overtime saw the Red Wings threaten the Ranger nets several times without success. Now they were in the second overtime and there was a faceoff near the Ranger goal.

George Gee was pitted against Buddy O'Connor at the faceoff. Moments earlier, Gee had been shouting at Pat Egan of the Rangers. Egan had accused him of "fainting" or begging for a penalty when he

Team captain Sid Abel, who scored a goal in the Red Wings' win, hoists the Cup for the newspaper photographers.

Gordie Howe, who led Detroit to the Stanley Cup, was unable to play in the Finals.

was knocked to the ice.

"Shut up, you big so-and-so," yelled Gee, "you'll be on the ice, Egan, when we get the winning goal."

Gee asked Babando to change position a few feet, to stand directly behind him, rather than at an angle. Babando shifted.

The puck was dropped. Gee hooked it and flipped it to the rear, to Babando. In one smooth motion the forward blasted the puck toward the net. It sailed a few inches inside the pipe, to the left of the goalie.

"I didn't aim, I just banged it," said Babando.

It was the second goal of the night for Babando, who only recent-

ly had been sitting on the bench.

Babando came to Detroit in the Quackenbush trade. He won a regular position, then broke a bone in his hand. Other players took over his job, and he never really became a regular again. Some fans and players wondered if his morale had been broken.

For the last two playoff games, however, Babando was back at the old stand. He played stoutly. In the biggest game of all he was the hero.

Detroit's comeback exploits are well known. They won two straight games to avoid elimination against Toronto. They did the same thing against the Rangers. They went an entire season without dropping a "really important" contest.

To vanquish the Rangers on Saturday and Sunday they twice were forced to wipe out early two-goal leads, a feat extremely difficult under playoff conditions where tight defensive play is standard.

New York scored its first two goals (Allen Stanley and Tony Leswick) during Detroit penalties. Babando and Abel tied it at 2-2 within a 21-second spell during a Ranger penalty. The third goal for each club was made under full-strength conditions.

All of the original scoring was packed into the first two periods. With the score 3-3, there followed 52 minutes of shutout hockey.

Then Babando broke the spell and won the Stanley Cup.

HOWE & CO. CRUSH ALL-STARS

Red Wings Power Past NHL's Best, 7-1

By Paul Chandler

The Detroit News

All of the opponents had spies in the rink, so it's certainly no secret now. The Red Wings look maybe 15 percent better than a year ago, when they won everything.

If they aren't four or five games ahead of the National Hockey League race by Christmas, then everything that happened at Olympia Sunday night was a dream — a bad dream for the rest of the league.

ALL-STARS

1

RED WINGS

7

Detroit,
Oct. 8, 1950

Coach Tommy Ivan's 1950 Detroit team swept up the ice with the NHL All Stars, 7-1, before 11,058 spectators, giving the picked team its first defeat in four annual games.

Ted Lindsay, 10 pounds heavier and three steps faster than last spring, lashed three goals in the net for the first hat trick in All-Star game history.

Terry Sawchuk provided the snappiest goaltending ever seen in the annual game, losing his shutout through a teammate's defensive mistake 90 seconds from the end of the game.

Gaye Stewart and Metro Prystal, obtained from Chicago by trade, gave a new, pleasing look of depth to the forwards. Prystal smashed home the most difficult goal of the night, crashing headlong into the boards after making a diving shot. He was stunned, but not hurt.

Gordie Howe was smoother and trickier than a year ago. He got a goal, too.

"We'd better get in shape fast," most of the All-Stars muttered in their dressing room, "because these guys are ready."

Manager Jack Adams had a gleam in his eye, but he did caution, "We simply were in better shape, far better shape. Our problem probably is not to get down too fine."

This was the first time the Red Wings had faced Jack Stewart as an opponent, and it was a sorry night

Playing on home ice, Gordie Howe and the Red Wings demolished the NHL's All-Star team.

for Black Jack. He was on the ice when five of the goals were made — on four of them his defense partner was Bill Quackenbush.

It was the first time the Red Wings had attacked Walter Broda since the playoffs, and Old Turk was slow. He gave up five of the team's seven goals.

A check of writers and officials from the five other clubs found only one delegation, Toronto, expressing any kind of confidence about their team this season. And the Maple Leaf people added, "of course, everything depends on Broda, who's 36 now."

RED WINGS END RANGERS' HOPES

Sawchuk in Vezina Trophy Lead

Special to The Detroit News

Only one long screened shot got into his cage as Detroit defeated New York, 4-1, here Wednesday night, but Terry Sawchuk still lost ground in the Vezina Trophy battle.

Sawchuk's lead was whittled to a single goal because Al Rollins of Toronto recorded a 2-0 shutout over Montreal. Sawchuk now has yielded 136 goals, compared to 137 for Rollins and Turk Broda of Toronto. Both clubs have two games to play.

Detroit's victory, featuring three assists by Red Kelly and goals by George Gee, Doc Couture, Sid Abel and Ted Lindsay, removed the Rangers' last chance of making the playoffs.

But it's still anybody's guess whether the Red Wings first-round opponent will be Montreal or Boston. The Bruins beat Chicago, 6-5, while the Canadiens were losing and today they're one point apart — with two games to go. Les Canadiens have the benefit of the

RED WINGS

4

RANGERS

1

New York,
March 21, 1951

extra point and also the advantage that if the battle ends in a tie (in points) they will be declared the higher team because of a greater number of victories.

Shortly after New York faded from the scene, Frank Boucher said he would keep his promise to resign as manager if the team failed to make the playoffs.

Playing before a small crowd of 5,837, Sawchuk's chances of a shutout went fleeting before five minutes had elapsed. Buddy O'Connor put the puck in the net from about 50 feet out, with a crowd milling in front of Terry.

Detroit now travels to Montreal for a game Saturday before returning to Olympia for the last contest at Olympia Sunday, against those same Canadiens.

The Red Wings, who won the Stanley Cup in 1950 and '52, kept the Rangers out of the playoffs with their 4-1 win.

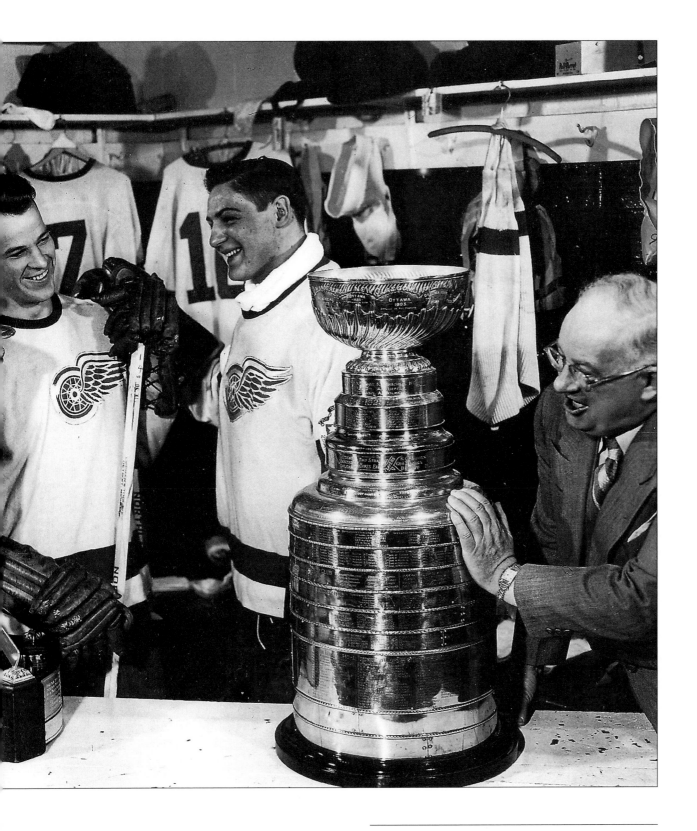

WINGS ACCLAIMED THE 'GREATEST TEAM'

Detroit Dominates in Sweeping Montreal

By Paul Chandler

Special to The Detroit News

Somehow, when a person thinks about it, it doesn't seem right that the three biggest men on the Montreal team should be sulking bitterly in their dressing room at the exact moment the Detroit Red Wings are being hailed by thousands as the most dazzling of modern hockey teams.

How can one sulk when he has been ousted in four consecutive games, when the opposition has so many resources and you so few, when a rival goalie has allowed only two goals in four games, and your team has been blasted out of the Stanley Cup Finals by the score of 11-2?

Throughout the hockey empire there are experts who today will swear that there's never been a team to equal this one, which blanked the Canadiens, 3-0, before 14,545 last night to seize the Stanley Cup in the breathless span of eight straight games.

Hockey is a hard game of stresses and strains, like football, and temporary loss of form is routine. Never before in the history of the Canadian sport has a club been able to start at high speed and keep accelerating enough to win every single game as it arrived — eight victories in eight visits to the ice.

CANADIENS

0

——

RED WINGS

3

Detroit,
April 15, 1952

Where on a single team have there been so many shooting experts? You stop Gordie Howe and Ted Lindsay and Sid Abel and what happens? Something like this final game when Metro Prystal came out of the pack to flash the puck twice behind Gerry McNeil, and his linemate, Glen Skov, made another goal. Neither had entered the playoff goal column previously.

How often will any club, however brave, encounter a goalie like Terry Sawchuk has been this season? In most ways, no team ever has had to combat such a guy before. During the entire playoffs, Terry's home crowd didn't see a puck get behind him once — four straight shutouts on Olympia ice, he gave the local fans.

In the eight games he yielded five goals, an average of about one every five periods. Only two goalies ever have finished a playoff with four shutouts behind them, and Dave Kerr needed nine games to do it, while Frank McCool used 13 games to get his name in the records. To the average citizen, then, these will seem like extraordinary feats, the cumulative products of the persons and elements that constitute the 1952 Detroit hockey champions. With the world turning as uncertainly as it always has, the exploits might not be duplicated for many years — though the Detroit club has all the signs at the moment of one that can be held together for some time.

But to three men from Montreal — Coach Dick Irvin, Maurice Richard and Elmer Lach — the joy of Detroit was not to be watched with grace. They ran for their dressing room, ignoring the time-respected custom of rivals meeting and shaking hands on the ice at the finish of a series, and ultimately they hurried out a side

Terry Sawchuk allowed only two Montreal goals in the Stanley Cup Finals.

door of the stadium without a word to the conqueror.

"Have your fun," Irvin shouted sourly to the spectators who hooted at him from the jammed corridors after the game. He then bolted his dressing room door against the Detroit press.

Ah, but some of us fooled the canny Canadien. The Montreal reporters were told of Irvin's remarks, and one of them disclosed that he had said:

"You can't win hockey games without scoring goals."

It was not revealed whether he

criticized those of his players who did take the opportunity after the game to skate down and hug and handshake their opponents of the moment earlier — all Montreal players except Richard and Lach did this.

Well, however the sullen threesome feel about it, Detroit fans are not gloating excessively. Montreal came into the playoffs with a tired, broken club, shot with big injuries and meeting a strong, rested opponent who nursed a wounded pride suffered when upset in the playoffs last season.

As ignored as it is by many who govern hockey, the 70-game regular season proves certain things. When considering that Detroit whipped Montreal four-in-a-row in the playoffs, it must be noted that the Red Wings would end the season 22 points ahead of the Canadiens; that Detroit lost only two of 14 meetings to that particular rival in a whole winter.

Detroit figured to win the round decisively, and it did it only sightly faster than expected. There's never been a round that went so according to form.

Sawchuk says he was more at ease in the final game than in any of the previous seven. "I don't think I had as many hard chances, either," he said, "and somehow I never had an idea that any would get through. Everybody up front was playing too well."

His teammates got him a goal a period. Prystal blasted from 20 feet, dead

The Red Wings gather around to admire the Stanley Cup, which they won after a hard-fought series with Montreal.

in front of the net, during a penalty to the moody Richard in the first period. Johnny Wilson and Alex Delvecchio had wrestled for the puck and eventually shoved a pass toward him.

Late in the second period, Prystal tossed a pass toward Skov, who was floating in the pivot lane before the net. Gaunt Glen slapped it low to a corner.

Midway in the third period, Prystal poked a puck from Paul Meger's stick, and, lo, there he was with clear pathway down the ice — the Montreal goal 130 feet in the distance.

Prystal raced, picked up the puck, and roared in alone, firing hard and high when he got to within 15 feet. It made a big bulge in the back of the net.

Many persons have figured in making the Red Wings of 1951-52 successful, and in this narrative the name of Coach Tommy Ivan has not yet appeared.

He is the blender and ran virtually the perfect bench through the whole year. A player revealed last night that in his pregame instructions, Ivan had tapped his kid line of Prystal, Wilson and Delvecchio on the shoulder and implored them, "The way this lines up tonight, you three guys could win the Stanley Cup for us."

As it happened, that particular line made all of the goals.

Ivan was asked if he was a prophet. "Naw," he said, "I just thought the Canadiens had a weakness, that's all."

Metro Prystal and Glen Skov scored two of the Red Wings' three goals against the Canadiens.

The Red Wings swept Montreal, 4-0, in the 1952 Stanley Cup Finals.

LINDSEY SCORES 4 GOALS – WINGS MAKE IT 10

Detroit Buries Boston, Clinches Playoff Spot

By Harry Stapler

Special to The Detroit News

Hockey is called the fastest of pro sports. Often it's so fast that fans can't tell how goals are scored.

Even goalies can't always tell. The best authority is the man who scored them. In this case the authority is Ted Lindsay, the lithe, little Red Wing forward who tallied four times last night (first time he ever got four in a single game).

Here is how each goal looked from (1) eyes of most of the 10,973 Olympia Stadium fans, (2) eyes of Ted himself, and (3) eyes of Jim Henry, the tired Boston Bruin goalie who suffered through the Red Wings' 10-2 victory:

Fans — Suddenly No. 7 (Lindsay) gets the puck in front of the net and whips his arm. The red light doesn't glow. No. 7 flicks his stick again. The red light glows at 7:22 of the second period.

Lindsay (in the dressing room afterwards) — "Marty (Pavelich) dug

BRUINS

2

RED WINGS

10

Detroit,
March 2, 1953

the puck out right behind the net and slipped it out to me in front of the net. I shot and Henry stopped it. The rebound came back to me and Henry was down on the ice. I flipped it over him into the top corner."

Henry — slumped beside a trunk in the Boston dressing room — "Was that in the first or second period?"

Fans — No. 7 and No. 9 (Gordie Howe) streak toward the net. No. 9 shoots. The goalie stops it. No. 7 sweeps in. The red light shows at 15:48 of the second period.

Lindsay — "Marty gave me the puck at the blue line. I gave it to Gordie and followed him in as a trailer. Gordie shot and the rebound came back to me, Henry was off-balance and I picked the far corner."

Henry — "Y'know, I don't think I was ever more tired."

Fans — This time they know for sure. No. 7 skates in fast from the right side and shoots from 12 feet. Red light shines at 19:01 of the second period.

Ted — "I broke through the cen-

ter and Gordie hit me with a perfect pass. The puck sort of rebounded off my stick ahead of me. Racing after it, I more or less shot at it back hand. I'm not sure how it got in. It had a prayer on it. I thought it went between Henry's legs but Metro (Prystal) said it went in on the long side."

Henry — "These long road trips sure are hard on you."

Fans — No. 7 and No. 9 race from mid-ice together against two defensemen. No. 9 doesn't shoot, instead feeds the puck to No. 7 who is uncovered. A 25-foot shot. Red light at 13:15 of the third period.

Lindsay — "Gordie put me in perfect. All I had to do was beat Henry and I did it on the short side."

Henry — (Silence).

One-sided it was, but the Red Wings' victory had some other noteworthy aspects:

The league-leading Wings clinched a playoff berth and at least a tie for second place. Five more victories in the remaining 10 games will cinch first place, no matter what happens to Montreal.

Howe scored his 43rd goal on a

Ted Lindsey scored four goals in one game against the Boston Bruins. It was a first for him.

40-foot, flick-of-the-wrist shot in the second period. That, combined with three assists, gives him 85 points for the season, one short of the record he set himself. He still needs seven to tie the goal-scoring record.

The Wings scored eight straight points before the Bruins tallied early in the third period (NHL record in one game is 15 straight).

Benny Wolt played in his 60th game for the Wings and scored his first goal when his 55-foot shot bounced off the skate of Bill Quakenbush into the net. In addition, Red Kelly got his 17th goal and Alex Delvecchio, Marcel Pronovost, and rookie Marcel Bonin scored.

RED WINGS GAIN NOT ENOUGH

Maple Leafs Outshot, But Get 0-0 Tie

Special to The Detroit News

Detroit benefited by the scoreless tie with the Toronto Maple Leafs here last night. While the Red Wings stayed five games ahead of second-place Toronto, they increased their margin over third-place Montreal to six games.

MAPLE LEAFS

0

RED WINGS

0

Toronto,
Feb. 17, 1954

Three games in five days are coming up.

It was the fifth scoreless tie for the Wings in two seasons. They played two scoreless ties with Montreal in the 1952-53 season and one with Chicago. This was the Wings' second scoreless tie with Toronto this season, duplicating the Jan. 3 game at Detroit.

For goalie Terry Sawchuk, it marked his 11th shutout of the season, putting him only one shutout away from his 1951-52 season record of 12.

It was the 10th shutout of the sea-

After the game, former Red Wings goalie Harry Lumley visited with Terry Sawchuk.

son for goalie Harry Lumley of Toronto. The latter thus maintained his two-goal lead over Sawchuk in the Vezina Trophy race, for the goaler whose team has the least number of goals scored upon it in a season.

While the 13,081 fans in Maple Leaf Gardens found it a very interesting game, it was a disappointing one to Manager Jack Adams. He

read the riot act to the Wings in a closed meeting before the game. He said he pointed out the Wings hadn't won a game from the Leafs on Toronto ice this season.

Adams has more ammunition to use on the Wings to get them keyed up for tonight's game with Dick Irvin's Canadiens and Maurice (Rocket) Richard, the erstwhile journalist. Four of the five players referee Bill Chadwick waved to the penalty box in the first period were Leafs. Yet not once were the Wings able to click on the power play.

The Wings outshot Toronto, 17-6, in the first period and had a 33-27 edge on the entire game. But only two penalties were called on the Wings, one each in the first and second periods, while Toronto had its fifth and last penalty of the game in the second period.

The Wings were missing aggressive Marty Pavelich, right winger on their starting line. Also missing was Al Arbour, the defenseman who was supposed to come up from Sherbrooke to replace Jim Hay.

Toronto's Harry Lumley maintained his lead over the Red Wings' Terry Sawchuk in the Vezina Trophy race, stopping 33 goals.

SMALLEST RED WING GETS BIGGEST GOAL

Leswick's Overtime Score Gives Wings the Cup

By Harry Stapler

Special to The Detroit News

Tony Leswick's right hand, the one that had swung the championship stick to trigger a sudden Stanley Cup celebration by the Red Wings, dialed the long-distance operator.

He was phoning his two staunchest fans, his small sons, Gary, 8, and Barry, 6. They had listened to a broadcast of the game 2,000 miles away in British Columbia, as had Lestwick's mother and father and a dozen relatives and in-laws.

Barry was on the line. His little voice shouted, "Daddy, you got a goal!"

Surely Daddy got a goal last night, probably the biggest one that the smallest Red Wing (5-feet-6 ½ inches) ever scored.

His goal at 4:29 of the first sudden death overtime period, won the game, 2-1. It also won for the Red Wings their sixth Stanley Cup championship in the seventh and final game.

For a moment after the goal, Gen-

CANADIENS

1

—————

RED WINGS

2

Detroit,
Sept. 16, 1954

eral Manager Jack Adams, who has been with the Red Wings for all their 28 years in Detroit, just sat in his box seat and looked out thankfully at the bedlam on the ice.

Adams' Wings, already the NHL champions for the last six seasons, had just won their third Stanley Cup in those six years. Hockey has never seen such dominance.

Leswick's goal (he said it was the first he had ever scored in overtime play) sent the Montreal Canadiens home beaten for the sixth time in the seven years they've collided with the Wings in the playoffs.

Leswick, seasoned by nine NHL seasons, was provided the overtime opportunity when teammate Red Kelly tied the score at 1-1 with a second-period goal.

Floyd Curry had pushed the Canadiens ahead in the opening period. It was a worrisome omen, for in all the earlier games of this series, the first team to score had always won.

Some mystery surrounded the closing events.

Leswick was 45 feet from the net, between the blue line and the right-hand circle when the puck reached him. But where did it come?

Leswick didn't recall the details. Glen Skov, who was credited with the assist, couldn't remember exactly what his part had been. Teammates told conflicting stories. In the press box, observers differed.

In the hysteria of victory, supplemental details grew hazy, perhaps to be cleared up later by the game movies.

Skov, whether he recalls it or not, apparently battled a Montreal player for the puck at the right of the net. The puck came out to Leswick, who took one quick step and swung. Montreal defenseman Doug Harvey said he tried to stop the goalward flight. The puck flicked off a desperate finger. That deflection fooled goaltender Gerry McNeil. Or so McNeil said. Gerry believes he would have stopped the shot otherwise.

When the three-inch disc passed over the goalie's right shoulder and hit the inside of the netting high up, 15,791 fans erupted into the noisiest moments in

After the Red Wings' win, Ted Lindsay (center) shares the Cup with Jack Adams and the Norris family.

Olympia's hockey history.

At least they should have been the noisiest moments for this was the biggest crowd ever to see a game at Olympia. For playoff drama, the scene had only one equal here.

On April 23, 1950, Pete Babando of the Wings scored a goal in the second overtime period to beat the New York Rangers in the seventh game and win the Stanley Cup for the Wings.

McNeil's known weakness is a high shot. Had Leswick taken advantage of this bit of intelligence?

"It's funny, but I didn't," grinned Tony as he drank champagne with his wife, Aunita, at the victory par-

ty in the Sheraton Cadillac. "I just shot as quickly as I could and it happened to go in high."

Leswick and his wife will soon head west to join their children at New Westminster, B.C.

Leswick's goal coming when it did is the thing they'll talk about. You might also converse about the other Red Wings. This was hockey at its finest.

Capt. Ted Lindsay played brilliantly despite an injury to his abdomen, an injury that he had glossed over and declined to converse about for several days. Lindsay fired the pass that set up Kelly's goal.

At the team party, Lindsay climbed

upon the dias represented by the base of the Stanley Cup and shouted, "A toast to the greatest competitor in hockey — Bob Goldham." Defenseman Goldham, 31, like Leswick, had smothered shot after shot before they could reach the Detroit goal.

Terry Sawchuk, never nervous, had guarded the Red Wing net tenuously. His steady play brought the Wings to the moment when Leswick produced. Sawchuk had been screened by two players when Curry's low liner went past him.

Kelly, the red-haired genius of skates, had to beat a defenseman and the goalie to score the tying one.

He neatly aimed the puck between the legs of the defenseman. McNeil didn't have a chance to stop it. The Wings had a one-man advantage.

Here are the 1954 names that will appear on the Cup, following the Canadiens of last year onto the 61-year-old piece of silverware donated by Lord Stanley of Preston. In the eyes of owners Marge and Bruce Norris, they are all heroes:

Kelly, Skov, Lindsay, Goldham, Sawchuk, Gilles Dube, Marcel Pronovost, Benny Wolt, Gordie Howe, Metro Prystal, Marty Pavelich, Alec Delvecchio, John Wilson, Earl Reibel, Bill Dineen. Al Arbour, Keith Allen, Jim Peters, Earl Johnson and, of course, Leswick. His name might be engraved in double-size letters.

Team captain Ted Lindsay savors the Wings' third NHL title in five seasons.

WINGS GET EARLY EDGE, SAWCHUK FOILS MAPLE LEAFS

Goalie Sparkles in Third Straight Shutout

Special to The Detroit News

In its hottest streak of the season, Toronto sought to replace the Detroit Red Wings in second place in the National Hockey League. But the Wings, in a bitter fight, managed to hold their own and win, 1-0.

RED WINGS

1

MAPLE LEAFS

0

Toronto, Nov. 13, 1954

Detroit had manpower advantages twice to once for the Maple Leafs in the first period. Goalie Harry Lumley robbed Lorne Davis, a Wings newcomer, of a goal the second time after spectacular saves on Len Kelly and Vic Stasiuk on the earlier penalty.

Goalie Terry Sawchuk sparkled for the Wings during the second period. He sprawled to block shots from Sid Smith and Eric Nesterenko, got his stick on a wicked backhander from George Armstrong and gobbled up a slap shot by Horton.

The Leafs' pressure evaporated when Nesterenko was thumbed for elbowing.

Terry Sawchuk shut out the Maple Leafs on their home ice.

HOCKEY'S FIRST FORFEIT – ALL GOALS STAND

Red Wings Can Clinch Championship After Victory

By John Walter

The Detroit News

Last night's forfeit victory over Montreal was only half the Red Wings' battle. The National Hockey League championship still will be decided when Montreal plays at Detroit Sunday.

Although nothing in NHL rules covers a forfeit, the 4-1 score and all statistics apparently will stand, because the Red Wings were ahead when rioting caused the game to be stopped at the end of the first period.

By winning, Detroit took a two-point lead in the standings, but Montreal can make up that gap by beating New York here tomorrow.

If the Canadiens beat New York, Detroit needs a victory Sunday to take the title — a tie would hand it to Montreal because it has scored more goals this season.

If the Canadiens tie or lose to New York, Detroit can win the title

RED WINGS

4

CANADIENS

1

Montreal,
March 17, 1955

with a tie Sunday. But regardless of tomorrow's outcome. Montreal can win the championship by beating Detroit.

Red Kelly and Dutch Reibel padded their individual statistics with two goals apiece in the brief game, while Red Wings goalie Terry Sawchuk perhaps benefited from the early close. By giving up only one goal to high-scoring Montreal (Calum MacKay got it), he fell only two goals behind Toronto's Harry Lumley in the competition for the Vezina Trophy.

While Sawchuk has only one more game, Lumley plays two — against Chicago and New York, both teams which like to play free-scoring hockey.

Maurice Richard, whose suspension fired the anger of Montreal citizens, also was aided. Neither Bernie Geoffrion nor Jean Beliveau, his close competitors for the league scoring championship, got either a goal or an assist.

Richard has 74 points, Geoffrion 72 and Beliveau 71.

The Red Wings were confident as they hurriedly left the Montreal Forum last night.

"I think we would have beaten them, 8-1, if the game had continued," defenseman Bob Goldham commented. "Montreal didn't have any spirit."

Kelly's first goal (at 5:05) actually bounced in off Montreal's defenseman Butch Bouchard. It was a 45-foot screen shot that Bouchard dropped to block, only to have it carom in the goal.

Six minutes later, Gordie Howe trapped Doug Harvey's pass at Montreal's blue line and shot the puck between Harvey's feet toward the net 45 feet away. Reibel wheeled as the puck came at him and back-handed it past Jacques Plante.

Kelly came up with his second goal while Detroit's John Wilson was in the penalty box for tripping. Marty Pavelich intercepted a Montreal pass and caromed it off the boards to Kelly, leaving him with only the goalie to beat.

After winning the Stanley Cup in 1955, the Wings capped a glorious run of four NHL titles in six seasons.

MacKay converted a pass from Ken Mosdell for Montreal's goal at 15:18, but three minutes later Riebel struck again while the Canadiens were short-handed.

Riebel's scores put him in a tie with Howe for fourth place in NHL scoring with 62 points. Kelly's 14th and 15th goals gave him 42 points.

100 Jailed in Wings Riot

Fans Turn Unruly After Campbell's Arrival

Special to The Detroit News

Thousands of revenge-crazed hockey fans went on a seven-hour rampage of destruction and looting last night and early today in the worst demonstration Montreal has seen since the anti-draft riots during World War II.

The fans, fired up to a fury of hate against the National Hockey League president, Clarance Campbell, smashed windows, looted jewelry stores and beat up innocent bystanders.

Their rage flared on long after a game between the Montreal Canadiens and Detroit Red Wings was called off at the end of the first period with Detroit leading 4-1. The game was forfeited to Detroit.

The riot started off as a noisy protest against Campbell's action in suspending Montreal's idol — Maurice (the Rocket) Richard — and grew until streetcar riders and persons walking along busy St. Catherine street cowered in fear of the frenzied demonstrators.

Passengers on streetcars, trapped near the Forum arena, lay on the floor as chunks of ice and bottles came smashing through windows, scattering glass and panic.

Police said they had more than 100 persons in custody as a result of the demonstration. Many of those seized had their pockets jammed with looted jewelry.

The mob went completely out of control, despite the efforts of hundreds of police and firemen.

Five of the demonstrators pounced on a taxi driver for no apparent reason and pummeled him with punches and kicks.

The mob toppled corner newsstands and set fire to others. Windows in more than 50 stores were smashed and a number of cars were overturned. Many people were injured, but none seriously.

Inside the Forum, there was a scene of hysteria as a fan tossed a tear-gas bomb into a passageway near the entrance, sending spectators choking and coughing through the exits.

Forum officials said only the calm of fans in the upper part of the rink, who retained their seats while those near the ice battled their way out, prevented a major disaster.

Campbell, the object of the fury, was punched in the face by one fan and nearly buried under an avalanche of overshoes, peanuts, programs, eggs, tomatoes and pennies. He said afterward, however, that he was unhurt.

By winning last night, Detroit took a two-point lead in the league race. However, Montreal has a chance to make up the margin by beating New York here tomorrow night.

The championship definitely will be decided when Montreal plays at Detroit Sunday night. Red Kelly and Earl Reibel scored two goals apiece for Detroit last night and Calum MacKay connected for Montreal.

The demonstration last night started innocently enough. Hundreds of fans jammed the lobby of the Forum two hours before game time but they seemed in a jovial mood.

However, when the game got under way and the efforts of those without tickets to crash the gates were repulsed by police, the crowd became more surly.

They assembled in a park opposite the Forum, and started hurling chunks of ice at streetcars.

Campbell's arrival midway through the first period touched off the demonstration inside by many of the 15,000 fans. For six minutes after his arrival he was pelted with programs and peanuts.

He took it all smilingly, as if he had expected it after setting down Richard for the rest of the season and the playoffs for a stick-swinging episode Sunday in Boston.

After a time, the demonstration subsided, but when the period ended with Detroit ahead, 4-1, the spectators renewed the barrage. This time, overshoes and bottles were added to missiles.

Ushers and police tried to keep fans away from where Campbell sat with three secretaries from NHL headquarters.

One spectator, however, pretended to be a friend of the league president and, with his hand extended as if to shake Campbell's hand, got through the guard.

He maintained the friendly attitude until he was within striking distance of Campbell and then slapped him across the face with his open hand. As Campbell fell back from the blow, the fan closed his fist and punched him.

Campbell retained his seat as police dragged his attacker off.

But when the tear-gas bomb was tossed into the passageway, Campbell joined the hundreds of other fans in putting his handkerchief over his face and heading for the exit.

Fire Director Armand Pare then ordered the game suspended, "for the protection of the fans." The order meant the contest was automatically forfeited to the Red Wings.

The cancellation seemed to increase the ire of the fans, who milled around outside for hours, throwing anything they could get their hands on at police, cars and streetcars.

When finally pushed back from the Forum the mobs marched up St. Catherine street, Montreal's main business artery, smashing windows and looting.

Police said it was impossible to estimate the amount of merchandise destroyed or stolen.

The outburst did not come without warning.

Since Campbell announced Richard's suspension for hitting Hal Laycoe of Boston with his stick and punching linesman Cliff Thompson, his office has been flooded with threatening calls, some warning that he would be killed if he went to last night's game.

Campbell accepted the dare yesterday afternoon and said that, unless police requested otherwise, he planned to attend.

No request came from police and midway through the first period, with Detroit ahead, 2-0, Campbell arrived at the Forum.

Last season, faced with almost the same situation after suspending Bernie (Boom Boom) Geoffrion for a stick-swinging affray with Ron Murphy of New York, Campbell did the same thing. After a few peanuts and programs were tossed at his arrival, the crowd subsided.

But this year, with Richard the central figure and with the championship hanging in the balance, there was no holding the frenzied Montreal supporters.

Instigators of the demonstration were still being rounded up today, but police said they had no hope of getting them all. Officers did not know who had thrown the bomb — a U.S. Army model.

After leaving the rink, Campbell went to the Forum clinic.

There, he met with Frank Selke, general manager of the Canadiens, and both signed a note and sent it to General Manager Jack Adams of Detroit in the Red Wings' dressing room.

It read:

"The game has been forfeited to Detroit. You are entitled to take your team on your way any time now. Mr. Selke agrees to this decision as the Fire Department has ordered the building closed."

Campbell remained in the clinic until 11:20 p.m., some two hours after the game was called.

Meanwhile, radio stations and newspapers were flooded with calls from persons who had heard he had resigned.

ADAMS DECLARES: 'MY GREATEST CLUTCH TEAM'

Detroit Takes Seventh Game from Montreal, 3-1

By Harry Stapler

The Detroit News

Once the bums of winter, the Red Wings are now the champions of spring. And in hockey, the springtime counts most. In becoming Stanley Cup champions again, the Red Wings beat the Montreal Canadiens, 3-1, last night in the seventh and final game.

The Wings again distinguished themselves before 15,541 — biggest Olympia crowd of the season — by winning when there was no room for losing. They've done it since early winter and they've done it most often to the Canadiens.

In the hockey empire, many people surely will call this the finest of many good Red Wing teams managed by Jack Adams.

"When some of these same boys were a little younger, we had teams that might have been better," said Adams. "But this bunch has 'em all beat on one score — it's the greatest clutch team I've ever had. They won every game that had to be won."

Adams and Coach Skinner pointedly avoided a long pep talk yesterday afternoon before the game. Among their economical sentences was: "There's only tonight — no tomorrow."

After the meeting the Wings rode from their Toledo hotel to Olympia in a bus.

"I know they're up," confided Skinner to Adams upon arrival. "They aren't saying a word."

One minute after the start, there was a hint. When Ted Lindsay, the team's obvious leader, was exiled to the penalty box, Detroit prevented Montreal from firing at the goal.

More hints followed. Montreal's feared Jean Beliveau and Bernie Geoffrion couldn't penetrate the so-called checking line of Marty Pavelich, Glen Skov and Tony Leswick.

Alex Delvecchio will be remembered for his two Red Wings goals and Gordie Howe for his one.

CANADIENS
1
_____
RED WINGS
3
Detroit,
April 14, 1955

Goalie Terry Sawchuk will be remembered for his near shutout of the Canadiens. Only Floyd Curry scored and that in the third period after the Wings led, 3-0. Sawchuk also will be remembered for stopping Ken Mosdell's dangerous shot in the game's first minute. If Mosdell had scored, the remaining 59 minutes might have changed.

The other 14 players should be equally commended. "You can't win a National Hockey League championship and a Stanley Cup without 17 players," said Bob Goldham. The Wings in third place in December, had won the NHL championship in a comeback that carried them through the Tear Gas Riot in Montreal to the final night of the regular schedule.

Expectantly, the crowd awaited the end. Would the Canadiens again refuse to congratulate the Wings? Last year the Montreal players brusquely skated off the ice after Tony Leswick's overtime goal won for Detroit.

They started away this time, too. But Bernie Geoffrion, who curious-

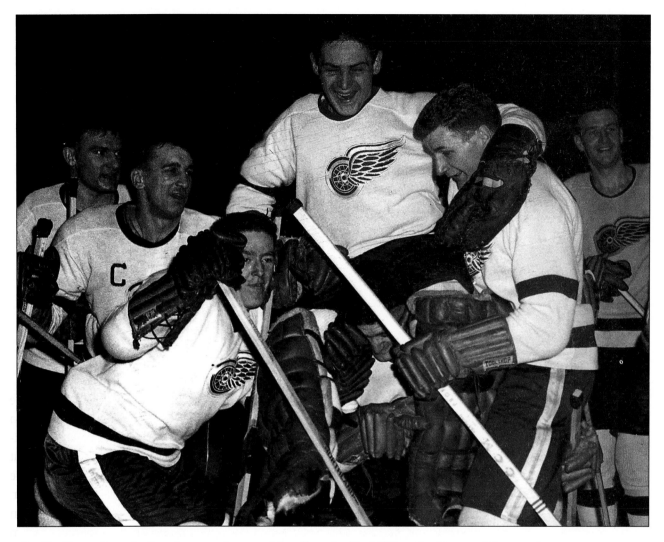

Goalie Terry Sawchuk enjoys a victory ride after the Red Wings' win over Montreal.

ly is the player the Wings chide the most, headed right for the Wings. Montreal's Tom Johnson saw Bernie moving and turned himself, reaching the Wings first.

Then other Canadiens returned to the ice to shake hands. Some didn't make it, notably Habs Coach Dick Irvin.

Jubilantly the Wings received the Cup on the ice. "Earlier in the season they called us bums and I guess it took bums to win," cried Lindsay to the crowd.

In the dressing room, the club terminated training rules and allowed beer for the players.

Later the celebration narrowed to a few hundred at the Sheraton Cadillac. Lindsay, as toastmaster, stood on a chair and dispensed champagne from the Stanley Cup. He especially praised Wings rookie coach Jimmy Skinner.

Now the Red Wings' count is seven Stanley Cups. They've won four cups in the last seven years. Also seven straight National Hockey League championships. How long can it last?

A Visionary Who Took the Wings to the Top of the NHL

Jack Adams' Teams Won Six Stanley Cups

By Joe Falls
The Detroit News

Jack Adams spent 50 years in hockey, 36 as boss of the Detroit Red Wings until 1963. He was combative, bold, brutally frank, big-headed and pig-headed. He was a man who had to have his way all the time.

He was also a very sweet man — a man who looked like Santa Claus himself with that red face, cherry nose and beaming smile. He could be as gentle and charitable as St. Nick himself. Mostly, he was a man with a big heart, a bit appetite and a big hip pocket.

The heart was how he ran his life — giving to others just when it seemed he was taking too much from them. He could anger you and please you in a matter of moments. You could get mad at him but it was hard to stay mad. He just wanted the best and didn't always know how to get it. The appetite was for life and all it offered.

They called him Jolly Jack because he enjoyed so much. He loved good food and good friends. He didn't drink or smoke. 7-Up was his drink, and he'd nurse them through the night as he sat in bars and taverns all across the NHL, talking hockey with his many colleagues.

His priorities in life were his wife, Helen, his hockey team and his friends. After the games, he'd come home and his wife was always up waiting for him, properly dressed as proper ladies do, even at these late hours. She was there to comfort him in the good times and bad times.

Their marriage lasted until Adams died, at 72, of a heart attack on May 1, 1968. He was at his desk working for the Central Professional League (soon to become the International Hockey League) when he collapsed. He didn't like the paper work but was still close the game he had loved for his entire life.

As for that big hip pocket, that's where Adams liked to keep people, especially members of the media. If they were on his side, they couldn't be against him, and he didn't like anyone to be against him. He would wine and dine the newspapermen and photographers who covered his team and did it in regal style, often hiring out entire restaurants and letting the good times roll until the last drink had been drunk, the last

Jack Adams played for both Toronto and Vancouver.

shrimp consumed and the last cigar smoked. Not everybody fell for his ploy, and Adams would be at odds with them on a steady basis, but most came around because they weren't making much money in their own jobs and enjoyed a good time as well as anyone else.

Remember: Jolly Jack liked everything going his way. The only one who ever got the best of him was Grant Warwick, a little forward for the New York Rangers.

One year, after the season was over, Adams took a team of NHL players on a barnstorming trip through Western Canada. These

might have been exhibitions, but not to Jack. That is, Not-So-Jolly Jack. When it came to hockey, everything was serious.

One night, the Red Wings played an exhibition game against the University of Michigan, and Adams didn't like the way one of his players had performed. When the evening was over, he gave the player a train ticket back to the minors. He never returned to the NHL.

So, as Adams' barnstorming team was making the rounds in Western Canada, not all of the players were giving it their best effort. It had been a long season and they felt this was time to unwind a little.

Not with Mr. Adams, you didn't.

He would be after them after every game, questioning their morals, their purpose, even their manhood. He would stand in the middle of the dressing room and start screaming at them the moment they came in off the ice at the end of game.

Not only was Adams a man of action, he was a man of many motions, waving his arms wildly, throwing orange slices at the players and kicking their sticks and skates around the room.

When he would start into one of these tirades, Warwick would leap from his chair in front of his locker and hold a camera in front of Adams' face.

"Hold it, Jack," he would say. "That's a terrific pose."

Adams would literally stop in mid-air, freezing like a stature in the park. Warwick would pop the flash and say: "That's a good one, Jack. You're really going to like it."

Adams would stop yelling and walk out of the room. Warwick did this through the entire tour, catching Adams in one absurd pose after another. He never told him there was no film in the camera.

As coach and general manager, Adams led the Red Wings to 12 league titles and seven Stanley Cups. In one span, from 1949 to 1955, the Red Wings finished first seven consecutive seasons. Not even the New York Yankees did that in their dominant years, nor did the Boston Celtics or Montreal Canadiens.

Adams used to bristle when his hockey team was compared to the Yankees.

"We are not the Yankees of hockey," he would say. "The Yankees are the Red Wings of baseball."

More than a motivator, more than a winner — even more than a con artist — Adams was an innovator. He always put the Red Wings first, but, because he loved the sport so much, he came up with many ideas on how to improve the game. He

Jack Adams was a hard-driving wing for Vancouver before returning to Toronto.

was the first man who had the ice cleaned between periods.

He did it after the Red Wings played the longest game in history — a 1-0 victory over the Montreal Canadiens in the Montreal Forum on March 25, 1936. The teams played 176 minutes and 30 seconds — nearly nine periods — and ended at 2:25 a.m. Adams felt the game dragged that long because the ice got so slushy.

He later saw attendants clean the ice between performances of an ice show in Europe and suggested to the National Hockey League that the same be done between periods of their games.

And the business of allowing only one goal to be scored on a power play also was Adams' idea.

The Canadiens went into Olympia Stadium for a game against the Red Wings in the late 1950's. This was when the Flying Frenchmen had an awesome power play. Playing one player up, the Canadiens scored two quick goals in the early minutes of play when Maurice (The Rocket) Richard put two pucks into the top of the net before anyone knew what was going on, effectively putting the Wings away.

Adams figured that was enough of that nonsense. He talked the other owners into adopting a rule where a team could score only once on any two-minute penalty.

Adams is remembered for developing those great teams of the late 1940's and early 1950's — powerhouses that featured the Production

Line of Sid Abel, Gordie Howe and Ted Lindsay. All are fabled heroes to this day.

But the Jack Adams story goes back, before he ever thought of coming to Detroit.

Born in Fort William, Ontario, on June 14, 1895, Adams learned to play hockey like most kids in Canada — in parks, on frozen lakes and pond and even in the streets when they iced over, which was often. They played 20 on a side, but that didn't matter. The trick was to learn to stick-handle so you could hold the puck for more than a few moments at a time.

Adams became so proficient at keeping the puck to himself that he became a pro player, a forward, for the Toronto Arenas, Toronto St. Pat's and Ottawa Senators, winning a Stanley Cup in Ottawa. He was tough and he could skate, taking no guff from any player on or off the ice.

In these early years he learned a philosophy about hockey that he taught for the rest of his life: "Knock the puck away from the man or knock the man away from the puck."

He came to Detroit and took over a floundering team named the Cougars in 1927. The Cougars played in Windsor in 1926 while Olympia Stadium was being built. The whole thing was a sad affair, with the Cougars winning only 10 games and finishing in last place.

More importantly, they lost $84,000 at the gate at a time when the first signs of The Great Depression were begin-

Jack Adams briefly coached Toronto and Ottawa before taking the Red Wings' job in 1927.

ning to be felt in the Detroit area.

Adams went in to see Charles Hughes, owner of the Cougars who was a prominent member of the Detroit Athletic Club. Adams played a heavy hand, knowing the man's plight.

He told him: "I won a Stanley Cup in Ottawa, so you need me more than I need you."

He got the job, no questions asked.

But the fortunes of the Detroit hockey team did not improve. The Cougars attracted only 80,000 for their entire first season in Detroit and the red ink ran all through

Olympia Stadium.

Even worse is that the fans booed the home team. Most of them were from Windsor, and they would cheer for the four Canadian teams that came to Detroit, especially the Toronto Maple Leafs.

One night, in 1930, the Cougars played a game for a charity run by Frank Murphy, the mayor of Detroit. It was strictly a cash deal. You could give anything you wanted for a seat.

Adams said: "Some guy drove down Woodward and showed up with five bags of potatoes. He wanted to see the game. We took the potatoes and gave him a standing-room ticket."

The depression left a deep mark on Adams. He said: "If we could get Howie Morenz from the Montreal Canadiens for $1.98, we couldn't do it."

In time, Adams was to sign a great goaltender for only $1.69. It was Sonny Eliot, the happy-go-lucky local weatherman who was a big fan of the Red Wings. It was the 1940's and NHL teams had no backup goaltenders, which meant they didn't have a second goalie if they ever wanted to scrimmage.

Eliot offered his services, even if he didn't know a goalie stick from a broom. They haggled over the price, and Adams grudgingly gave Eliot a contract for $1.69. In fact, he gave him a contract for $1.69 for the next 10 years or so, until the teams began hiring back-up goalies. The only exception was the year Adams —

remember, he looked like Santa Claus with those chubby cheeks — offered a contract for $25,000.

Sonny was stunned. That is, until he read the small print. Adams included a list of fines — showing up late, getting your uniform dirty, chewing bubble gum on the job, drinking beer at the Lindell A.C. and, of course, saying it would be nice when it rained.

The fines took the worth of the contract down to $1.69, a pact which Sonny happily signed.

Clarence Campbell, the President of the NHL, even endorsed the contract by putting his signature to the bottom of it. When he was finished coaching, Adams would sit in the press box, usually next to Eliot, and for Sonny it was like getting into the ring for a wrestling match.

Adams couldn't sit still. He was all over his seat, rocking back and forth with the ebb and flow of the game, putting elbows, arms and fists into Sonny's side and kicking him around the ankles.

"He put a few bruises on me, but how could you get mad a man who cared so much about his team?" Eliot said. "What I found funny is whenever one of his players would make a mistake on the ice, he'd look over his shoulder to see if Jack was in the press box watching."

Adams always expected top performances from all his players. When they stopped producing, he lost interest in them, sending them off to other teams.

The one thing he demanded was effort.

He hung a sign over the door leading from the dressing room and it hung there until the Red Wings left Olympia Stadium. The sign read: "We supply everything but the guts."

Adams could evoke feelings of fear and admiration almost at the same time. He could berate a player in front of the entire team, then slip him a $10 bill to have himself a good dinner.

Adams lived near the University of Detroit campus, and nobody knew him better than his butler, Joseph.

When the Red Wings would play at home on Sunday nights, Joseph would wait up for the master of the house. If he heard the tires on Adams' car screech as he turned into the driveway, Joseph would go upstairs and pretend he was asleep. He knew the Wings had lost.

If he didn't hear anything, he would meet Adams at the door with a cheery greeting: "Good evening, Mr. Adams. How did things go at the game?"

But it was faithful Helen who understood Adams the best. And when her man died in 1968, she maintained an immaculate house, with dinner on time every evening, as if Jack were still around.

But, of course, it was not the same. Too quiet. When Neil Armstrong landed on the moon in 1969 — just more than a year after

Adams' death — a kid from the down street, Gerry Coil, who was maybe six years old, showed up at the Adams home and rang the doorbell. He pulled a red wagon filled with rocks.

Helen went to the door.

"Good evening, Mrs. Adams," the boy said. "We are having a special sale this evening."

Mrs. Adams looked at the rocks.

"Really," she said. "What is it?"

"Moon rocks," the boy replied.

"How much are they?" Mrs. Adams asked.

"A nickel apiece but you have to buy two for 10 cents," the boy said.

"That seems a little high," Mrs. Adams said.

"They're straight from the moon," the boy said. "We just got them in today."

Mrs. Adams said: "All right. Let me get my pocketbook."

She returned to the front door, and boy gave her two of the rocks and she gave him a dime.

"Thank you, Mrs. Adams," the boy said. "I hope you enjoy your rocks."

When he left, Helen Adams closed the door and fell back against it. She looked down at the two rocks in her hands and said: "Oh, my! Two rocks for 10 cents. If Jack were here, he'd have gotten them for a nickel."

Jack Adams' Red Wings won six NHL titles in 36 seasons.

HAWKS' WIN INSURES COACH'S JOB

Chicago Wraps Up Cup with 5-1 Victory

By Bill Brennan

The Detroit News

Rudy Pilous and his burly Black Hawks, long the doormats of the National Hockey League, were to fly back to Chicago today with hockey's biggest prize — the Stanley Cup. And for the likable Pilous, a talkative, bushy-eyebrowed coach, last night's 5-1 Finals victory over the Red Wings at Olympia meant something much more than glory. It meant his job.

BLACKHAWKS

5

RED WINGS

1

Detroit,
April 16, 1961

Spirits were dampened slightly, however, when the Blackhawks reached Metropolitan Airport following the game and found their chartered flight grounded by the weather. After following the traditional ritual of drinking champagne from the massive silver cup in the dressing room, the Hawks settled for beer in the airport cocktail lounge, and returned downtown to hotels for the night.

Reports had circulated freely at the end of the regular season that it was "win or else" for Pilous, who managed Chicago to third place the last three years after a fifth-place finish his first year.

Chicago has long been the graveyard of coaches, and since the club entered the NHL in 1926-27, a total of 30 men, including Pilous, have guided the club.

With his job assured after eliminating the Red Wings, four games to two in the Finals. Pilous will be welcomed by a city that has waited 23 years to cheer a Stanley Cup champion. Not since the Cinderella team of 1937-38 have Black Hawk fans had that opportunity.

It is only the third time in history that the Black Hawks have won the trophy, which was worth $3,150 to each member of the Chicago team. Each player on the losing Red Wings squad received $2,150.

"Our extra weight told a bit and I would say it was the balancing factor," Pilous shouted, trying to make himself heard above the din of the Chicago dressing room after the victory.

The turning point in the game, the Chicago coach said, "was when (Reg) Fleming scored while we were shorthanded. It took the zip out of the Red Wings and gave us a lift."

Pilous was referring to Fleming's goal near the seven-minute mark of the second period which tied the score at 1. Detroit was storming Chicago goalie Glenn Hall with Black Hawk rookie Wayne Hicks in the penalty box when Red Wings center Len Lunde, attempting a long pass, put the puck on Jack Evans' stick. He broke into the Detroit zone and then Fleming intercepted another Red Wing pass after Pete Goegan, and Vic Stasiuk had regained possession.

Hank Bassen, replacing veteran Terry Sawchuk in the Red Wings nets, had no chance on Fleming's high, hard drive.

Twelve minutes later, Ab McDonald had the winner, tapping in the loose puck from outside the crease, where it lay after Bassen had made a tremendous save on Bobby Hull, who carried it in. When the red goal light went on, Detroit's hopes died.

For Detroit's Sid Abel, who like

Pilous was making his first appearance as a coach in the Stanley Cup finals, it was the disappointing end of a rough playoff.

"We ran out of gas," was his simple explanation. "Actually we lost the Cup in Chicago Friday night when they beat us there. We were up for that game and gave everything we had. For two periods we played the best hockey we ever played. Then the roof fell in and we ran out of gas in this one."

For the first 20 minutes last night it looked like the courageous Detroit club would force a seventh game. With Evans in the penalty box for Chicago, the Red Wings took the lead when Parker MacDonald jabbed the puck past Hall.

The goal was a tribute to the hockey genius of Gordie Howe, who stick handled the puck through three Chicago defenders before firing on the net. MacDonald stabbed in the rebound for his first playoff goal with teammate Bruce MacGregor standing at his side also jabbing at it.

With the roar of the partisan crowd of 14,328 urging them on, the Red Wings dominated the play for the balance of the period. Nursing its lead through the early minutes of the middle period. Detroit was trying desperately to add to it on its manpower advantage when Fleming changed it all with his goal.

Ab McDonald then added his goal before the period was over. Eric Nesterenko struck in the first 57 sec-

Chicago's Stanley Cup win saved Blackhawks coach Rudy Pilous' job.

onds of the final period for an insurance goal. Then Evans and Ken Wharram rounded out the scoring.

The goals by Fleming, Evans and Wharram were unassisted, coming on breakaways. And for Evans, his goal climaxed an outstanding playoff performance and was his first in two full seasons.

The rugged checking of Evans was hailed as the major factor in eliminating the defending champion Montreal Canadiens, who bowed to Chicago in six games. In the opening game of that series. Evans crashed Montreal's big Jean Beliveau into the boards and the high-scoring player went through the series without getting a goal. He entered the hospital right after the series, complaining of headaches.

But against Detroit, the rugged Evans and his hardchecking teammates found a worthy rival. Two Black Hawks, Murray Balfour and

Dollard St. Laurent, watched the final game from the sidelines with injuries. Balfour with a broken arm and St. Laurent with a jammed knee.

Detroit had its full squad, but defenseman Marcel Pronovost and Warren Godfrey were playing with injuries. Pronovost with a bad ankle and Godfrey with a sore knee.

And in the second period last night, the Red Wings lost Howie Glover, who suffered a bruised chest when checked by Chicago's Ron Murphy. Glover, who earlier in the series suffered an eight-stitch cut to his nose, tried to skate off after being hit but collapsed on the ice as he neared the bench.

In the same period, Chicago's Stan Mikita also had to be helped off when Red Wing defenseman Howie Young crashed into him just as McDonald scored the winning goal. Earlier in the period, Bassen was hit in the face by Tod Sloan's shot, but stayed in the nets after brief repairs.

LADY LUCK PLAYS A MAJOR ROLE AS LEAFS RETAIN CUP

Puck Bounces Right for Shack on Winner

By Bill Brennan

The Detroit News

A weirdly bouncing puck, rambunctious Ed Shack and Lady Luck collided in front of the Detroit Red Wings net last night and, because of it, the Toronto Maple Leafs are the proud holders of their second straight Stanley Cup, hockey's most- prized trophy.

The crucial collision came in the unlucky 13th minute of the final period of their playoff game before 14,403 screaming hockey fans. And with the goal Toronto broke a 1-1 tie that had existed from the opening minute of the middle period and went on to a 3-1 victory.

Rookie defenseman Kent Douglas had fired the hard shot from the blue line and the happy Shack later admitted in the noisy, champagne-soaked Toronto dressing room: "It bounced off so many players I lost count and then it hit my stick and went in."

RED WINGS

1

MAPLE LEAFS

3

Toronto,
April 18, 1963

It was the big goal of the night, but Lady Luck still had another role to play before the final whistle.

At 18:07 of the last period, Toronto's Bob Pulford drew a penalty for holding Alex Delvecchio and Detroit moved in with a desperate effort to stay alive in the best-of-seven series and force a sixth game. The Leafs had gone into the game with a 3-1 lead in the series.

With 45 seconds left and goalie Terry Sawchuk off the ice in favor of a sixth attacker. Detroit's Norm Ullman found himself in front of an open Toronto net with the bouncing puck at his feet. Ullman swung at the puck and flubbed a shot that bounced harmless off the legs of Gord Howe, who was sprawled on the ice with Maple Leaf goalie Johnny Bower.

It was the Red Wings' last chance. Shifty Dave Keon gathered in a loose puck after the next faceoff and from deep in his own end sent a long shot into the emp-

ty Detroit net for his second goal of the night.

"You need luck to win any hockey game and we had it on our side tonight," said Toronto coach Punch Imlach over the rim of a champagne glass. "I'm glad it's over."

In the equally noisy Detroit dressing room, the Red Wings hurriedly changed to catch a charter flight home.

They covered the disappointment of their defeat with the knowledge they had given the defending National Hockey League champions a tough fight.

Howe, who had been through it all before in his 17 years in the league, summed it up:

"When the puck doesn't bounce for you, it doesn't bounce. It's like spitting into the wind. You know you can't beat nature."

Then Howe, who had stayed on the ice while NHL President Clarence Campbell was presenting the historic trophy to Toronto Capt. George Armstrong, added:

"You know, while I was out there I took a swallow of their

After being defeated by the Maple Leafs, Gordie Howe (9) joins in a toast to the Stanley Cup champs.

champagne. If you can't beat 'em, join 'em."

The remark brought a laugh from the rest of the Red Wings, who had battled back into the game after giving up an embarrassing first-period goal to Keon while they had a man-power advantage.

With Toronto's Allan Stanley in the penalty box for elbowing Howe, the Red Wings were swarming in the Toronto end. Armstrong's clearing pass eluded Delvecchio at the Leafs' blue line and Keon outraced the Red Wing captain to beat Sawchuk with a rising shot.

If Delvecchio was guilty of a mis-cue on the play, he atoned for it in the first minute of the second peri-od when he tied the score by bang-ing a shot off the inside of the Toron-to goal post.

For the balance of the second period, both clubs played cautious hockey and went into the final 20 minutes of play with the spectators chanting for action.

And the noisy, partisan crowd fig-ured indirectly in Shack's deciding goal.

Frank Mahovlich, the player Chicago's Jim Norris had offered a $1,000,000 for at the start of the sea-son, skated off the ice before his turn was up and the fans booed him

loudly for giving the puck away at center ice. This brought Shack over the boards and the big, awkward skating forward was in the right spot seconds later when Douglas boomed his shot from the blue line.

From this point it was bedlam as the Red Wings killed off a penalty to Floyd Smith and then made their desperate bid for a tie and sudden-death overtime.

They failed, but their effort took its toll.

"I hope I never have to face that team again," said a weary Bower as he sat quietly in the corner of the jammed Toronto dressing room. "They skate too hard."

HOWE GETS RECORD AT LAST – THE HARD WAY

Shorthanded Goal Is No. 545, Best in NHL

By John Walter

Special to The Detroit News

Gordie Howe beat odds of better than 66-1 when he scored while his team was shorthanded to achieve the record-breaking 545th goal of his career in Detroit's crushing 3-0 victory over Montreal before 15,027 delirious fans at Olympia last night.

Goalie Terry Sawchuk extended to 132 minutes the time he has held the opposition scoreless as he counted his second straight shutout to tie the record for shutouts at 94 — set by the late George Hainsworth in $10\frac{1}{2}$ seasons with Montreal and Toronto (1926-36).

Significantly, the Red Wings' first victory over Montreal in three starts balanced off their victories against their defeats for a 6-6-1 won-lost-tied record. It also moved the Red Wings back into the thick of the National Hockey League race, dead-locking them with Toronto for third place at 13 points, only two points

CANADIENS

0

RED WINGS

3

Detroit,
Nov. 10, 1963

behind second-place Montreal.

National Hockey League records show that only four goals have been scored this season by the short-handed team in the 266 times the opposing team had a manpower advantage. Thus Howe, after suffering the embarrassment of hitting the post on a 60-foot shot at an empty net in the 1-0 victory over New York last Thursday, beat long odds in achieving "the-hard-way" goal that ended Maurice (Rocket) Richard's reign as the highest goal-scoring player in NHL history.

Montreal goalie Charlie Hodge, who Howe victimized for the fifth time in his career for his 545th goal, said he "played Howe all the way" and figured he had him covered on the short side of the net when the six-time scoring champion rifled the puck "about an inch off the ice" from 30 feet into a six-inch opening between the netminder and the left post.

"It was two-thirds of an inch off

the ice," Howe deadpanned in the Wings dressing room later. Then his face broke into a grin, a rarity for the 35-year-old Howe the last two weeks as he went five games without scoring after notching his 544th goal against Montreal's Gump Worsley on the Canadiens' last visit here.

Then Howe, who was playing in his 1,132nd game, gave his version of the play that delayed the game for seven minutes as the largest hockey crowd at Olympia in 22 months gave him a thunderous ovation.

Manager-coach Sid Abel had sent Howe out in the second period to help kill off the five-minute major penalty called on Alex Faulkner when he accidentally nicked Montreal's Ralph Backstrom for a two-stitch cut over the left eye. Barely eight minutes earlier, Faulkner had matched Bruce MacGregor's goal 51 seconds previously to give Detroit a 2-0 lead.

"Marcel Pronovost dug the puck out from the boards," related Howe, "as (Billy) McNeill and I circled in our end.

" 'Let's get going' I yelled at McNeill. I noticed the Montreal players weren't going back. (Bill) Gadsby wheeled and we had a 3-on-2 break."

Only (Jacques) Laperriere and (Jean) Beliveau were back.

"I passed ahead to McNeill who veered toward the center of the rink with Gadsby driving down left wing. Billy gave it back to me. Hodge appeared to move out a little, cutting down the angle. I shot for the short side."

Howe fired from 30 feet and Hodge threw his left leg sideways belatedly, causing him to sprawl on the ice at the corner.

Howe teetered on one skate as he swirled behind the net, and then fell to one knee. McNeill was right after him, dropped to both knees and gave Howe a bear-hug. They knelt there for a moment before fellow players cascaded on them, including Faulkner, who jumped out of the penalty box.

"I feel 10 pounds lighter," Howe said to Abel when he finally leaned against the boards as maintenance men started cleaning up the debris, even as the ovation continued.

The logical play for McNeill was to pass to Gadsby who was wide open on left wing. Abel said afterward, since Hodge was covering the short side. Why did McNeill pass to Howe, instead? McNeill explained:

"As I was going over the blue line Gadsby yelled for the puck. Beliv-

Gordie Howe's 545th goal surpassed Maurice (Rocket) Richard's NHL all-time scoring record.

eau and Laperriere seemed to move that way. So I passed to Gordie behind me, instead. He let loose (with his shot) right away."

Thus Howe — picked as the league's most valuable player last season for an unprecedented sixth time — foiled the strategy of Montreal coach Toe Blake. The latter had converted Jean-Guy Talbot from a defenseman to left wing for the night, with instructions to shadow Howe.

Gilles Tremblay shadowed Howe so successfully on Montreal's previous visit, he had only two shots. But he scored on his second shot. When

a mix-up on the Canadiens' bench left them momentarily two-men short. This time Tremblay was out of the lineup with a broken cheekbone. Worsley was sidelined with a pulled hamstring muscle and Bill Hicke with a concussion.

That's why Talbot was pressed into service as a forward and Blake had rookies Wayne Hicks, Bryan Watson and Claude LaRose doing partial relief duty in the Canadiens' lineup.

However, the Wings took charge early with the brace of goals by MacGregor (his first in 10 games) and Faulkner (his fourth).

ULLMAN, PRONOVOST HAILED IN WIN OVER CHICAGO

Rout of Blackhawks Forces Seventh Game

By Bill Brennan

The Detroit News

Norm Ullman and Andre Pronovost might be a surprise to the Chicago Blackhawks, but, as far as Sid Abel is concerned, the two hard-skating forwards are doing what comes naturally.

Ullman paced the fired-up Detroit Red Wings to a 7-2 rout of the Blackhawks last night with a three-goal "hat trick," his second of the Stanley Cup semifinal series. The lopsided victory deadlocked the series, 3-3, and forces a seventh and deciding game in Chicago tomorrow night.

Pronovost, Ullman's linemate who also teams with the veteran center as Detroit's penalty killing combination, also scored last night to run his series goal output to four, which ties him with Gordie Howe.

Ullman, Provnovost and the rest of the Red Wings admitted they were

BLACKHAWKS

2

RED WINGS

7

Detroit,
April 7, 1964

aroused because of the disputed goal in Sunday's game in Chicago, which they insist cost them the game. The Hawks won it, 3-2.

That goal and the resulting dispute also cost Abel, the Detroit manager-coach, a $500 fine by Clarence Campbell, the National Hockey League President.

Abel was notified just before game time of the fine, which resulted from his blast at referee Frank Udvari. He called the referee "gutless" and accused him of "stealing the game" when Udvari ruled that Ken Wharram had scored before he had blown the whistle in a jam-up around the net. The goal tied the game in the third period, and then Stan Mikita scored later for the Chicago victory.

The Detroit coach was high in his praise of Ullman and Pronovost in the steaming, noisy Red Wings dressing room after last night's game. He said they had played terrific hockey throughout

the series and didn't need anything to fire them up.

"Normie's no surprise to me," said Abel. "He had a terrific second half during the regular schedule and he's just keeping it up.

"With Andre, it's a little different. He went 29 games before he scored in that last one of the season against Toronto ... and that's the kind of guy that generally gets hot in the playoffs. We were mentioning it before the series started that Pronovost would likely get some big ones for us. He's always a hard skater ... and not they're going in for him."

The Wings feel confident they can KO the Blackhawks tomorrow to go on to meet the winner of the Montreal-Toronto semifinal, which is also deadlocked at three victories apiece.

It is the first time in the history of the National Hockey League that both semifinal series have gone the limit. The last time a playoff series went seven games was in the semifinal between Boston and Toronto in 1959, with the Leafs winning.

The teams played almost on even terms in the opening period last night with Terry Sawchuk, still nursing a throbbing shoulder from a pinched nerve in his back, making several key saves.

After trading power-play goals in the first period, the Wings erupted to put four past goalie Glenn Hall, who was replaced in the Chicago nets at the start of the third period by rookie Denis DeJordy. An ailing stomach hampered Hall during the first two periods.

Chicago got its second goal in the middle period and that was it for the night for the Blackhawks during the first two periods.

Chicago got its second goal in the middle period and that was it for the night for the Blackhawks. The Red Wings added to the rout by scoring twice on DeJordy in the final period, once while killing a penalty and another on a power play.

The Wings scored three goals while they had a man-power advantage as referee Art Skoy called a total of 16 penalties, eight against each club.

Ullman opened the scoring in the game, deflecting the puck past Hall. Wharram then tied it, lifting the puck over Sawchuk from a scramble in front of the goal.

Ullman and Marcel Pronovost teamed to feed Howe the puck for a Detroit goal shortly before the two-minute mark. Howe blasted the puck between Hall's pads and that

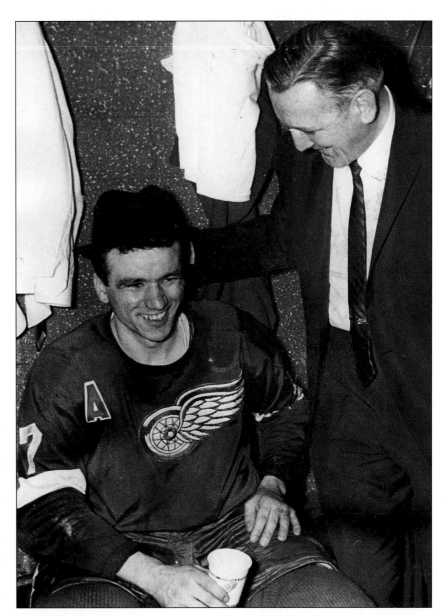

Norm Ullman's "hat trick" lifted the Red Wings past the Blackhawks in Game 6 of the Stanley Cup semifinals.

one broke the tie and the Red Wings never looked back.

Parker McDonald got Detroit's next goal, also on a power play with Chicago's Eric Nesterenko in the penalty box. His goal-mouth shot hit the inside of the goal post after teammate Floyd Smith knocked Hall's big leg pad out of the way with his stick.

ULLMAN'S 3 GOALS RIP BLACKHAWKS

Second-Period Scores Come 5 Seconds Apart

By Bill Brennan

The Detroit News

Norm Ullman is making a habit of scoring three-goal "hat tricks" against the Chicago Blackhawks and the silent Detroit Red Wing veteran does it in dramatic fashion.

The 30-year-old center established a new National Hockey League record in the heat at Olympia last night in leading Detroit to a 4-2 victory over the Blackhawks, a triumph that gave the Wings a 3-2 edge in the best-of-seven semifinal series.

A year ago, when the Wings eliminated Chicago in seven games in the semifinals, Ullman turned in a pair of hat tricks.

He got the first one in the second game to pace Detroit to a 5-4 victory that tied the series at a victory apiece and he gained his second one in a 7-2 rout, which knotted the series at 3-3.

With the Hawks leading, 2-1, at the 15-minute mark of the middle

BLACKHAWKS

2

RED WINGS

4

Detroit,
April 11, 1965

period last night, Ullman went to work and scored the fastest two goals in NHL playoff history.

The goals came five seconds apart on identical 50-foot slap shots and the feat erased the old mark of seven seconds, which was set last year by Chicago's Bill Hay against the Wings. Ironically, Hay could almost be described as the "goat" when Ullman established his record last night. The teams were playing five-a-side with Chicago's Stan Mikita and Detroit's Warren Godfrey in the penalty box when Ullman connected.

On each scoring play, Ullman faced off against Hay. On the first one, he took the puck on a pass from Detroit defenseman Bill Gadsby to drift over the Chicago blue-line and snap a shot along the ice that went between Hawk defenseman Pierre Pilote and Elmer Vasko and lodged in the corner of the net at goalie Glenn Hall's left.

After the goal, referee John Ashley faced off at center ice and Ull-

man won the draw from Hay, but the puck bounced to the boards where Chicago's Eric Nesterenko picked it up.

The Hawks forward attempted to pass it to Hay, and Ullman intercepted and snapped another shot along the ice, this one beating Hall on his right side.

With his third goal, Ullman was even more dramatic. There were two minutes left in the third period with Detroit's Gordie Howe in the penalty box when Ullman gathered in Godfrey's pass while Chicago was caught changing lines and beat Hall with a shot from just outside the crease.

The goal brought a standing ovation from the crowd of 15,007, sweltering in the stadium heat and it sealed the victory for Detroit.

The series now shifts to Chicago for a sixth game tomorrow night and back to Olympia if a seventh game is needed.

Chicago coach Billy Reay thinks it will be.

"This series will go seven games," he declared, trying hard to hide his disappointment at the defeat.

For a while it appeared that it was going to be a disastrous night for Detroit, but the Wings came from behind twice to secure the victory.

Nesterenko scored Chicago's first goal in the opening period just 18 seconds after Detroit defenseman Marcel Pronovost got out of the penalty box.

With 41 seconds left in the period, 39-year-old Ted Lindsay deadlocked the score when he tipped in Gary Bergman's blue-line drive while Chicago was playing a man short.

The scored remained tied until the 15-minute mark of the middle period when Bobby Hull, Chicago's one-man team, turned a penalty into an asset.

The 25-year-old Hull was given a two-minute minor penalty for boarding Larry Jeffrey, and he leaped on the ice at the end of his penalty just in time to take a pass from Doug Mohns at center ice and go in all alone to beat goalie Roger Crozier.

Hull faked the Detroit rookie once before rifling a six-foot shot into the net. It was his seventh goal of the series and his tremendous contribution can be better evaluated when it is realized that his club has scored 15 goals in the five games compared to Detroit's 17.

"I thought we were outplaying Detroit until that goal outburst by Ullman," Reay said dejectedly. "We had them hanging on the ropes, but Ullman's second goal got them back

Norm Ullman's "hat trick" led the Red Wings to a 4-2 victory.

in there and I can't take anything away from them because they held us off in the third period ... I have to give them credit for that."

Detroit coach Sid Abel was careful to avoid any series victory predictions, but observed, "I

thought we played just as well as they did, except for a few minutes at the start of the game. We were taking good bites out of them all night because it was a hard-checking game."

For goalie Hall it was a nightmare.

'Wings Deserved to Win'

By Jerry Green
The Detroit News

Answers to questions raised as the Red Wings again went ahead in their Stanley Cup semifinal series with a 4-2 victory over the Chicago Blackhawks last night:

Did the heat — it was about 90 degrees in Olympia and steam arose from the ice surface — tire the Hawks, who combated the Red Wings with three lines against four?

Coach Billy Reay: "No, I don't think so. The difference was they got a couple of 50-foot goals."

What about the third period — Detroit seemed to be strong while Chicago seemed to wither?

Reay: "Detroit deserved to win the way they played in third period."

Norm Ullman didn't do so well in the Red Wings' two losses in Chicago. But he got those two long goals, the tying and winning ones last night. Did the Hawks do something different to try to neutralize Ullman in Chicago than they did in Olympia?

Reay: "Who said Ullman played

Norm Ullman scored the two fastest goals in NHL history — just five seconds apart.

that well? You can't judge a guy as having a good game on those kind of long goals."

Reay changed his first line — the Bobby Hull-Phil Esposito-Chico Maki

combination — around constantly in the last two periods. First, Camilla Henry moved in at left wing with Hull replacing Esposito at center. Then, Dennis Hull took over and Henry returned to the bench. What was wrong?

Reay: "Esposito's back started acting up again. I tried Henry and then Dennis because I was trying to help things and sometimes changes like that do the trick."

In the second period, goalie Glenn Hall reached for a high shot at Chicago's goal by Alex Delvecchio. Then he called time. Why?

Hall's pants were falling down. Stretching for the puck, he broke his suspenders. Before the game the Red Wings plus two goalies out for the warmup. That's one above the limit. Why the extra man?

Coach Sid Abel: "I had both Val Fonteyne and Murray Hall out with the idea that one would be scratched before the game. Fonteyne had a good warmup after his injury so he played and Hall was scratched."

WINGS BOW; HOWE GETS NO. 600

Worsley Gives Up Another Milestone Goal

By Bill Brennan

The Detroit News

For the third time in his 20-year National Hockey League career, Gordie Howe victimized goalie Gump Worsley to chalk up a milestone goal.

He did it Saturday night when he scored in the final period for his 600th regular-season goal. Despite the fact it represented a fat round figure to the Detroit Red Wings veteran, it seemed to excite him less than the crowd of 14,956, which gave him a standing ovation.

The crowd had something else to cheer about, too. They watched the Montreal Canadiens skate to a 3-2 victory over the Wings.

The victory boosted the Canadiens into a first-place tie with Chicago, and the defeat sent the Detroit club tumbling into the NHL cellar behind the Boston Bruins, who beat the Maple Leafs, 2-1, in Toronto.

Howe's big goal came shortly after

RED WINGS

2

CANADIENS

5

Montreal,
Nov. 27, 1965

the 16-minute mark of the third period with Detroit trailing, 3-1.

Gilles Tremblay and Yvan Cournoyer had scored first-period goals for the Canadiens and Norm Ullman and Bob Rousseau had added third-period goals before Howe connected.

Scoreless for his previous five games, Howe has been fond of picking on Worsley for the big goals. He scored No. 500 against him on March 14, 1962, when Worsley was playing for New York.

Howe then tied Maurice (Rocket) Richard's record of 544 on Olympia ice in Detroit when he beat Worsley in the third period on Oct. 27, 1963.

Saturday night, Howe's big goal was a pretty one. He took a pass from Gary Bergman from the corner and then flipped the puck into the open side.

Detroit offered only sluggish opposition to the Canadiens in the opening period and gave up two goals. Tremblay scored the first one

three minutes after the opening whistle. The first of two penalties to Detroit defenseman Warren Godfrey opened the way for Montreal's second goal — a strange one.

Goalie Roger Crozier left his net to clear the puck from the side of the net when it deflected high and landed at the corner of the goal where Cournoyer tapped it in.

In the middle period, the Wings showed more hustle but failed to score. Two penalties were called in the period by Referee Frank Udvari. However, neither club could take advantage of its opportunity.

Ullman brought some life into the Wings' attack near the midway point of the final period when he teamed with defenseman Doug Barkley to beat Worsley.

The veteran Detroit center — a 42-goal man a year ago — picked up his sixth goal of the season when he fired Barkley's rebound into the open corner of the net.

Bergman, who reported to the Wings Saturday after being recalled from the Central Hockey League team at Memphis, had to be helped

Gordie Howe scored his 600th goal in the final period against Montreal.

off the ice minutes later when John Ferguson crashed him into the ice.

Rousseau then gave Montreal a two-goal lead when he picked up a stray puck at the blue line and skated in to beat Crozier.

Then came Howe's milestone 600th goal and the crowd gave him its ovation and littered the ice with debris causing a five-minute delay while the big right winger was cheered to the bench.

The cheers for Howe turned to boos in the final minutes, however, when he drew a major penalty for high sticking J.C. Tremblay. Then Bruce MacGregor and Jacques Laperriere drew minor penalties, and it was over shortly afterward.

The thud was the defending league champion Wings dropping into the NHL basement.

In the dressing room, Howe showed more elation than he has on the ice.

"Maybe this will take the pressure off both me and the club," Howe said. "I hadn't been feeling the pressure on this until recently when everybody started talking about it."

Detroit manager Sid Abel echoed Howe's statement.

"I'm glad its over ... now maybe we can settle down and play some hockey. The pressure is off."

TAINTED GOAL WINS CUP FOR CANADIENS

Wings Rally, But Lose as Richard Scores in OT

By Bill Brennan

The Detroit News

Montreal is again in possession of the Stanley Cup today, but the goal that retained hockey's most prized trophy for the Canadiens is a topic of a raging debate.

CANADIENS

3

RED WINGS

2

Detroit,
May 5, 1966

Henri Richard was credited with the confusing goal, which came at 2:20 of the first overtime period last night at Olympia and defeated the Detroit Red Wings, 3-2, in a game that must go down as a Stanley Cup classic for hard play, determination and excitement.

Trailing, 2-0, midway in the second period after Montreal goals by Jean Beliveau and Leon Rochefort, the Wings stormed back to force the sudden-death overtime on a power-play tally by Norm Ullman and a third-period goal by Floyd Smith.

Then at the 2:20 mark, Richard collected his tainted goal — his only one

The Canadiens rush Roger Crozier in the Detroit goalmouth.

Montreal scored on a 3-on-2 rush on Henri Richard's controversial goal.

in the playoffs — without a shot being fired, either by himself or Dave Balon, who had carried the puck in on a 3-on-2 break with linemates Richard and Rochefort. Balon fell when he tried to get his shot away and skidded with the puck toward goalie Roger Crozier, who blocked the puck and Balon.

Balon bounced up and Richard, who also had fallen, came along on the ice in front of the net with Gary Bergman, the Red Wings defenseman.

Then the puck was in the net.

Stunned disbelief gripped the crowd

of 15,154 in the jammed stadium.

All was silent for a second. Then bedlam broke loose, and an ink bomb stained the ice near the Wings' net while debris bombarded players from both teams and teen-agers swarmed over the boards.

Clarence Campbell, the President of the National Hockey League, could do no more than hand the trophy to Beliveau, the Montreal captain, in the melee. He had no opportunity to make a presentation speech after the Canadiens won their fourth

straight game after losing the first two in the best-of-seven series.

The angry Wings, after brief handshakes of congratulations, clomped to their dressing room with bitter blasts at referee Frank Udvari.

Crozier, who was voted the outstanding player of the playoffs and received the Conn Smythe Trophy and the accompanying automobile and $1,000 cash prize declared.

"Richard threw the puck into the net with his hand. If Udvari was on top of the play like he's supposed to be, instead of staring into the crowd, he'd of seen it."

Defenseman Gary Bergman: "Richard couldn't have knocked it in with his stick because I had a tight grip on it with one hand ... He had to knock it in with his hand."

Detroit manager Sid Abel: "It was a helluva way to lose a hockey game. Both my guys claim Richard threw it in."

Referee Udvari: "It was a legitimate goal. Bergman had flipped Richard in front of the net and they were both sliding toward the goal. Richard seemed to be protecting his head with his arms and Bergman had a grip on his stick when the puck bounced out off Crozier and hit Richard and bounced into the net.

"I don't think Richard realized it had gone in. But if the Wings were unhappy with the call, why didn't they protest? It was a terrific game and it's too bad that it had to be settled by a goal like that."

Said linesman John D'Amico: "When the puck bounced out after Crozier made the stop on Balon, it hit Richard on the side or the leg and went in. That's the way I saw it."

Said Richard: "I was lucky ... but the puck bounced in off my leg."

Udvari, who called five penalties against the Wings and two against the Canadiens, including a misconduct to Jim Roberts, was not quite accurate when he said the Wings didn't protest.

Crozier chased Udvari almost the entire distance to official timekeep-er's desk arguing the goal, but the referee kept shaking his head.

Among the veteran hockey men in the press box it was described as — the cheesiest goal ever to win a cup."

Abel agreed.

"I'm proud of my guys — every one of them — and they deserved a better fate. They had Montreal hanging ... especially in that final period."

Montreal's Toe Blake, who is hockey's most successful Stanley Cup coach with seven trophies in 11 seasons, was sympathetic to Abel's view.

"I feel sorry for the other team," Blake said. "They played so hard to win before their home fans. To lose like this is not only discouraging to them, but also to their fans.

"When we scored our first goal, I thought that would slow them down. Then when we scored our second goal to go two up I was sure they'd quit but they didn't.

"Then they forced it into overtime and while we were waiting for the overtime period to start. I didn't say a word to my players. They were too tensed up. They knew what they had to do. It was a great game."

It was. And it started that way from the opening faceoff. The Canadiens, however, had a slight edge in the play and Claude Provost scored for Montreal just before the eight-minute mark, but the goal was called back by Udvari when he ruled the play offside.

Ninety seconds later, however, Gilles Tremblay got behind rookie Detroit defenseman Bert Marshall to set up Beliveau, who scored from a difficult angle.

Then in the second period, Rochefort scored midway in the period when Richard set him up with a hard pass and Crozier had no chance.

Montreal defenseman Ted Harris was penalized seconds later for interfering with Smith and, while the Wings had the manpower advantage, Ullman deflected Alex Delvecchio's hard blast from the point. The puck sailed high into the net behind goalie Gump Worsley.

It wasn't until halfway through the third period that Smith scored the tying goal to force the game into overtime. Defenseman Gary Bergman, who played his finest game of the season, fired a blistering shot from the point, which Worsley managed to sprawl in front of. The puck bounced off Worsley, hit Smith on the knee and sailed into the net.

The entire third period belonged to the Wings and only spectacular saves by Worsley, prevented the Detroit club from going ahead. He made big saves on Delvecchio, Andy Bathgate, Dean Prentice, Bryan Watson and Gordie Howe before the period ended.

The save on Howe, which came with less than three minutes left in the period was sensational with the plump goalie getting only his toe of the hard shot to steer it wide of the net.

Then came the overtime with its heartbreak, for Detroit. But it is a safe bet the goal will be argued until the new season opens next October.

HOWE BORROWS STICK, GETS NO. 700

MacGregor Gets 'Assist' in Landmark Goal

By Bill Brennan

The Detroit News

One of Bruce MacGregor's hockey sticks is on its way to the Hall of Fame in Toronto to be put on display in a place of honor in hockey's shrine.

The reason is simple. Detroit's durable and fabulous Gordie Howe borrowed it last night and scored his 700th regular-season National Hockey League goal.

The milestone goal, which came at 7:13 of the first period, fired up the Red Wings and Detroit went on to route the Pittsburgh Penquins, 7-2, while bombarding Pittsburgh goalie Les Binkley with 50 shots — their highest output of the season.

But why borrow one of MacGregor's sticks?

"Because the last batch they sent me were horrible," the 40-year-old Howe answered. "The shaft of Brucie's stick is not as flexible, although I would still like a stick with a stiffer shaft."

RED WINGS

7

PENGUINS

2

Pittsburgh,
Dec. 4, 1968

Then Howe, who is now playing in his 23rd NHL season — all with the Wings — added:

"I'm glad it's over."

Munching on a chocolate bar while he talked, Howe said, "I must feel 10 pounds lighter ... that's why I'm eating this bar."

The scoring play was started by linemate Frank Mahovlich, who took the puck away from Charlie Burns, a former Detroit player, behind the Pittsburgh net and passed it up to Alex Delvecchio along the boards.

Delvecchio whipped the puck to Howe, who was standing 20 feet out from the net and slightly to Binkley's right. He worked the puck on his forehand and whipped it along the ice into the far corner of the net.

"I didn't even look when I took the pass from Frank," Delvecchio explained. "I knew Gordie was out there in that general area and I just threw the puck.

"Now we can play hockey again," the team captain added with relief.

"Before, we were always thinking about it ... and they were accusing us of feeding the puck to Gordie ... I don't think we were, but we were accused of it anyway."

In a lighthearted mood after the game, Howe laughed when asked if the shot went where he intended it go.

"Sure, into the net," he said. "Seriously, I didn't have much time to think on the shot ... I just snapped it along the ice."

For a milestone goal, it was wasted on the skimpy crowd of 4,414 in Pittsburgh's Civic Arena. Most of the fans stood up and cheered when referee Ron Wicks dug the puck out of the net and handed it to Howe. However, there was no delay and play resumed immediately.

The goal pulled the Wings into a 1-1 tie after Keith McCreary had opened the scoring for Pittsburgh. Then the Wings went to work and, before the period was over, MacGregor also using one of his own sticks, gave Detroit a 2-1 lead. Nick Libett later added a pair, with Garry Unger, Bob Baun, and Danny

Gordie Howe, who scored his 700th goal against Pittsburgh, was often forced to outmuscle his opponents.

Lawson collecting singles.

Billy Harris scored Pittsburgh's second goal on netminder Roger Crozier early in the third period.

"I'm not sure whether Gordie's goal loosened us up or not, but it certainly appeared to do it," Wings coach Bill Gadsby remarked. "I know it helped Gordie because he confessed to me before the game he was feeling tense and tight."

Gadsby had praise for all three members on the line, and singled Mahovlich out for a special pat on the back.

"He started it all when he got the puck away from Burns," Gadsby said.

Because the Wings come right back tonight to play the first New York Rangers in Olympia, the Detroit coach rested his Production Line of Howe, Delvecchio and Mahovlich for much of the final period.

"After the 10-minute mark in the final period, I didn't use Baun either," Gadsby remarked. "We've got a lot of hockey ahead and a big one with the Rangers. I wanted them rested."

Taking the 2-1 lead into the second period, Libett and Unger scored to boost the lead another two goals.

Then in the final period, while the Wings were blasting 23 shots — another season high — Baun, Libett and Lawson scored.

"What I liked to see was those Libett, Lawson and Unger getting goals," Gadsby said. "That's what we must have ... and this was a big game for us. We had to have it."

The victory increased Detroit's record over expansion clubs to four victories, three losses and three ties. After playing the Rangers tonight, the Wings take off on a four-game road trip, including a swing to the West Coast.

MAHOVLICH LEADS RED WINGS OVER SEALS

'Big M' Scores Four Goals in 5-1 Rout

By Bill Brennan

The Detroit News

Frank Mahovlich is again the "Big M," the smooth skating left winger that the Chicago Black Hawks' late Jim Norris once tried to buy from the Toronto Maple Leafs with a certified check for a million dollars.

In the Detroit Red Wings' 5-1 victory over the Oakland Seals at Olympia last night, Mahovlich proved again why he has such strong appeal to the fans in the National Hockey League.

With the effortless grace that is almost his trademark, the 30-year-old left winger scored a pair of goals in the opening period and singles in the second and third.

Gordie Howe scored the other Detroit goal with the Production Line of Mahovlich, Howe and Alex Delvecchio living up to its name in giving the Wings their fourth straight win.

With his spree, Mahovlich now has run his goal total for the season to 25

SEALS

1

RED WINGS

5

Detroit,
Jan. 12, 1969

— tops on the Wings. It was also the third time this year that he has scored three or more goals in a game and it was the third time in his NHL career that he has had a four-goal night.

"I've been trying to think about the other two times I scored four," Mahovlich said in the dressing room after the game. "I'm sure I had them both back in 1961 ... that was the big year."

It was. That year Mahovlich scored 48 goals while playing with the Leafs on a line with Red Kelly (now coach of the Los Angeles Kings) and Bob Nevin (now with the New York Rangers).

The last few years, however, Mahovlich's goal production fell off. In 1966-67, he had 18 goals. Last season, before he, Pete Stemkowski and Garry Unger were traded to the Wings for Norm Ullman, Paul Henderson and Floyd Smith in March, he had scored 19 goals for the Leafs.

There had long been reports that Mahovlich and Toronto Manager-Coach Punch Imlach

couldn't get along.

That appeared to be the case because in the 13 games he played for Detroit to wrap up last season's schedule, he scored seven goals for a total of 26 for the year.

Now he has 25, one shy of his total output of a year ago. He also has 13 assists for a total of 38 points.

The tall left winger now has scored six goals in Detroit's last three games and last night's batch came with a forehand drive, two backhanders and a tap-in of a rebound.

He scored the four goals on the first five shots he had on Oakland goalie Charlie Hodge. He had another two shots later and nearly upped his total, but Hodge made big saves.

Frank Mahovlich (right), along with Gordie Howe and Alex Delvecchio, formed the famed Production Line.

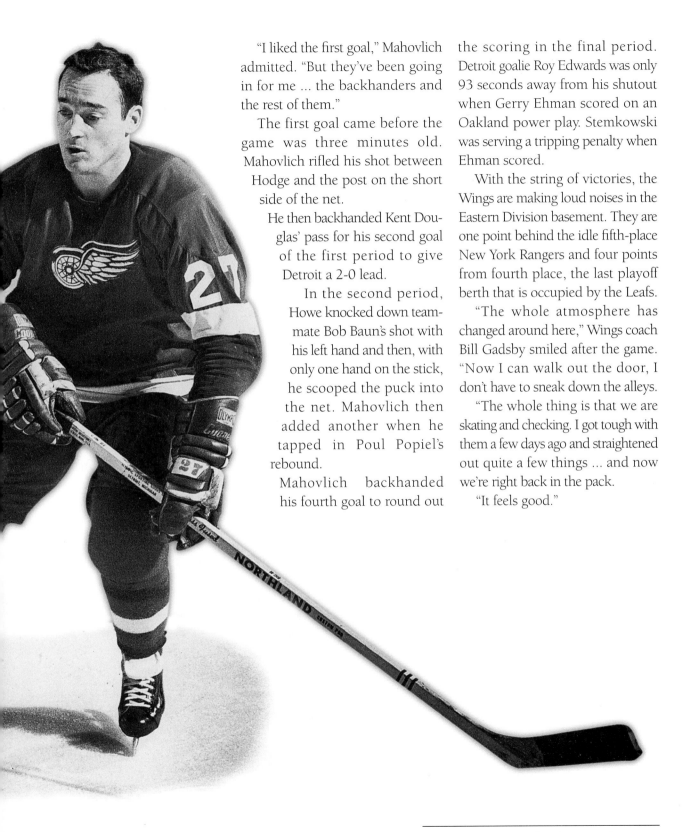

"I liked the first goal," Mahovlich admitted. "But they've been going in for me ... the backhanders and the rest of them."

The first goal came before the game was three minutes old. Mahovlich rifled his shot between Hodge and the post on the short side of the net.

He then backhanded Kent Douglas' pass for his second goal of the first period to give Detroit a 2-0 lead.

In the second period, Howe knocked down teammate Bob Baun's shot with his left hand and then, with only one hand on the stick, he scooped the puck into the net. Mahovlich then added another when he tapped in Poul Popiel's rebound.

Mahovlich backhanded his fourth goal to round out the scoring in the final period. Detroit goalie Roy Edwards was only 93 seconds away from his shutout when Gerry Ehman scored on an Oakland power play. Stemkowski was serving a tripping penalty when Ehman scored.

With the string of victories, the Wings are making loud noises in the Eastern Division basement. They are one point behind the idle fifth-place New York Rangers and four points from fourth place, the last playoff berth that is occupied by the Leafs.

"The whole atmosphere has changed around here," Wings coach Bill Gadsby smiled after the game. "Now I can walk out the door, I don't have to sneak down the alleys.

"The whole thing is that we are skating and checking. I got tough with them a few days ago and straightened out quite a few things ... and now we're right back in the pack.

"It feels good."

HOWE SHAKES OFF THE YEARS, NETS HAT TRICK

40-Year-Old Has More Goals Than Ruth Has Homers

By Bill Brennan

The Detroit News

Life begins at 40?

The Chicago Blackhawks think so.

In fact, there is not a dissenting voice in the rest of the National Hockey League when it comes to 40-year-old Gordie Howe, who is now less than two months away from his 41st birthday.

The durable Howe was as spectacular as he has even been in his 23-year career with the Detroit Red Wings while scoring a hat trick in pacing Detroit to a 6-1 victory over the Blackhawks last night.

The victory was an important one for the fourth-place Wings. It moved them three points ahead of the Hawks and the idle Toronto Maple Leafs, who share last place. The Hawks, however, have played one less game than Detroit, and the Leafs have played four fewer than the Wings.

With the three goals, Howe ran his season total to 28 and his career total to 716.

BLACKHAWKS

1

RED WINGS

6

Detroit,
Feb. 6, 1969

Along the way last night he eclipsed Babe Ruth's home run total of 714, a milestone borrowed from another sport because Howe has run out of them in his own. Ironically, or appropriately, Howe passed Ruth on what would have been the late slugger's 74th birthday.

When Howe scored his 700th regular season goal on Dec. 4, the curator of Hockey's Hall of Fame at Toronto was on hand to claim the stick.

Howe did all his scoring in the first two periods after Dean Prentice launched the Wings on their way to the crucial victory with a goal before the game was two minutes old.

Before the opening period ended, Howe picked up his first goal. Then, after 23 seconds of play in the second period, Frank Mahovlich scored his 32nd of the season. Howe followed this with goals No. 27 and No. 28.

Howe's first goal of the second period came while Dennis Hull was off with an interference penalty. It took the Wings just six seconds to connect after referee Bill Friday sent the younger Hull to the penalty box.

Chicago, badly outplayed the entire game, scored before the second period ended when Ken Wharram spoiled the goalie Roy Edwards' bid for a shutout with a high shot.

Bruce MacGregor added Detroit's final goal in the third period one second after a penalty to Chicago's Stan Mikita expired.

Howe had taken part in that Detroit power play, and it was his last appearance on the ice for the night. Wings coach Bill Gadsby elected to rest Howe for the remainder of the game because Detroit plays the Hawks in Chicago tomorrow night.

"He asked if I wanted a rest when I came off after that power play and I told him 'no,'" Howe said. "He told me, 'You'd better take a rest anyway. I really didn't want to, but maybe it was the best thing to do.'"

The rest may have deprived Howe of a four-goal night, one of the few thrills he has never experienced in his NHL career

---

Gordie Howe (9) scored three goals in his record-setting game against Chicago.

although last night's hat trick was his 17th. When Howe scored his third goal — a shot that goalie Dave Dryden partially blocked only to have it trickle into the corner of the net — the sellout crowd of 14,630 gave the right winger a standing ovation.

The ovation was accompanied by several felt hats tossed on the ice.

For the Hawks, the defeat was a costly one in the race for the fourth and last playoff berth and it also pointed up a glaring weakness on the Chicago defense. In two nights, the Blackhawks have given up 13 goals while scoring three.

With the Wings skating hard and checking hard, Chicago managed only 17 shots on Edwards for the 60 minutes. In only three through to the Detroit net and the first came 11:04 of the period.

The Wings bombarded Dryden with 43 shots, 19 of them in the final period.

"We were moving tonight," Gadsby acknowledged. "When you hold a team to 17 shots and get yourself, you must be doing something right. Now if we just come back and do this again tomorrow night ... if we can ... "

Gadsby's right. It would certainly give the Wings a more comfortable grip on fourth place.

Howe Led the Way and the Wings Followed

No. 9 Remains Hockeytown's No. 1 Hero

By Joe Falls
The Detroit News

This happened in Toronto. They had a kids team in town named the Red Wings and somebody thought it would be a good idea to bring them to Maple Leaf Gardens to meet the real Red Wings, who were to play the Leafs that night.

The kids were brought into the Detroit dressing room to meet the players. Gordie Howe was a little late because of a TV appearance. When he showed up, one of the officials pointed to the young boys and said: "Look who's wearing No. 9."

There was a Chinese boy of about 10, and his cheeks turned to crimson. Howe saw the boy's embarrassment. He stuck out his hand and said: "So you're Polish, too."

The boy's smile lit up the room. No. 9.

This was the true measure of the man.

They said he was a dirty player. He'd give you an elbow in the corner or the butt end of his stick and you'd leave the ice dripping blood.

True.

But so many people missed the point. Gordie Howe never went after anyone — certainly not to hurt them just to hurt them. He was retaliating. Always retaliating. If you did something to him that he felt was unfair, he would get you. Maybe not on this shift, the next shift or even before the game was over. But he would even up things, even if it took a week, a month or next season.

He was so strong, especially from the waist up, that he could out-muscle anyone in the National Hockey League. He could also out-play them, and it would not be incorrect to call him the greatest player of all time.

Gordie Howe, who was a scoring phenom, checks an opposing wingman into the boards.

He was tough and gentle at the same time, and if you knew him at all, his kindness far outweighed his toughness.

He liked to play his little games with people.

One night a heckler in the stands got all over him. Howe took it for a while, pretending not to notice, but when the moment was right, he skated by the boards and reached into the seats and nicked the guy's nose with the tip of his stick. No harm done. No blood. But the poor guy could feel the sting the rest of the game.

If you wanted to interview Howe after a game, it helped if you wore an armor suit. He did not like talking about himself — still doesn't, in fact, as he nears 70.

When you approached him in the dressing room, he would shoulder you into his locker.

It hurt but not so much to be painful. He knew just how to apply the pressure. He would put a soft elbow into your ribs and, with great dexterity, grab your ... well, you figure it out ... and give a little squeeze.

That was enough to send you staggering away, trying to maintain your dignity while searching for someone more peaceful, such as Alex Delvecchio or Marty

Pavelich or goalie Terry Sawchuk, who was merely off on one of his screaming spells.

The smile never left Howe's face. No. Make that a leer. He was the little boy who did something behind his mother's back and got away with it.

Where do you begin with his accomplishments? He played until he was 52 years old — 26 years with the Red Wings (1946-1971) and four years with the Houston Aeros of the World Hockey Association (1973-1976), two with New England of the WHA (1977-1979) and one with Hartford of the NHL (1980).

He came out of retirement so he could play with his two sons — Mark and Marty — in Houston. Some thought it was a foolish gesture for such an old man. In his first game with Houston, Howe scored in the first minute of play.

"It took Marty and I only two weeks to catch up with the old man," grinned young Mark Howe.

When Howe played in the NHL, he got into 1,687 regular-season games and had 786 goals, 1,023 assists, 1,809 points and 1,643 minutes in penalties — all league records at the time.

It was his charm off the ice which drew so many people to him. When he suffered a near-fatal head injury in the playoffs in 1950, he was left with a blinking

At age 17, Gordie Howe played for the Omaha Knights, a Detroit farm club.

condition. When he got out of the hospital, he said: "The next time I go on television, I think I should tell the viewers that the blinking is not the fault of their receivers ... it's me."

Howe was always joshing around with those he liked, particularly members of the media. If he was fond of a photographer, he would lob a puck into the seats where the guy was shooting pictures and drop in right in his lap. A souvenir for the guy's kids.

One time, in the middle of a game, Howe skated to the side of the rink and asked Roy Bash of The Detroit Times where he would like the puck to go into the

net on his next goal.

"The lower left corner," said Bash, who trained his camera on that spot.

Within minutes, Howe put the puck right there and Bash got his shot for the night.

Howe was born in Floral, Saskatchewan, where his father was a garage mechanic. Young Gordie began skating at the age of three.

It wasn't easy. The temperatures would drop to 50 below, but he was always out there, trying to stand up straight on his skates.

"As a kid, the only equipment I had were my skates and a stick," Howe recalled. "I took magazines and mail-order catalogs and stuck them in my socks for shin pads. I tied them together with rubber bands made from inner tubes. We played with tennis balls instead of a puck. The ball would get so hard from the cold we'd have to get new ones all the time. A woman next door used to warm them up in an oven for us."

Howe quit school and got a job with a construction company that was building sidewalks. It was hard work — lugging 85-pound cement bags — but it firmed up his muscles. Construction work, though, was just a fill-in between hockey seasons.

"I guess he always knew he was going to be a hockey player," said Howe's mother. "He used to prac-

The Production Line (left to right) — Gordie Howe, Sid Abel and Ted Lindsay in their early years.

tice at night under the city lamp on the streets. I put papers on the kitchen floor so he wouldn't have to take off his skates when he ate."

Howe almost wound up playing for the New York Rangers.

When he was 15, he packed a shirt, a set of underwear and a toothbrush in a little bag with his skates and took an overnight train to Winnipeg, where the Rangers were in training. He was scared stiff being away from home. He was a big kid for his age but was frightened when he saw the big-league players.

The veterans like to liked to haze the newcomers and they kept swiping Howe's dinner plate. All he was left with were his knife, fork and spoon. He didn't say anything. He simply sat there and didn't eat.

Alfie Pike, one of the veterans and a man who would become coach of the Rangers, saw what was going on and said: "OK,

guys, that's enough. Give him back his plate."

Young Gordie took it sheepishly, saying nothing and eating with his head down. They gave him all kinds of equipment to wear but he did not know how to put the stuff on.

"I just dropped the gear on the floor in front of me and watched the others," said Howe. "I found out pretty soon that the best way to learn was to keep my mouth shut and my eyes open."

He became homesick when a friend was cut from the team. Young Gordie left the camp a few days later, figuring his career was over before it started. But the Red Wings came along and invited him to their camp in Windsor. They could see the potential in him. They could certainly see that quickly developing body.

Jack Adams assigned Howe to the Wings' junior farm team in Galt, Ontario. They wanted him to go to Galt High School, but, when Howe saw so many kids jammed around the front door of the school, he walked down the railroad tracks and applied for a job with Galt Metal Industries as a spot welder. He never minded tough work.

After scoring his record-545th goal, Gordie Howe visits with the press in the locker room.

When Howe joined the Red Wings in 1946, it was clear he was a young man of tremendous talent. Just as he did as a kid, he was able to keep the puck to himself in practices. His stickhandling was uncanny and he frustrated players who had been in the game for years.

Sid Abel, one of the older veterans, went to Howe one day and said: "I don't mind this great stickhandling of yours, but why stickhandle around the same player three times?"

It turned out Howe was a great athlete, as well as a great hockey player.

He could hit the ball a mile on the golf course and keep it reasonably straight. He once played with Chick Harbert, the reigning PGA champion, and outdrove him on every hole.

Howe always wanted to try his hand at baseball. He told this to Lou Boudreau, the manager of the Cleveland Indians, and when the Indians came to Detroit to play the Tigers, Boudreau invited him out to batting practice. To give him a proper test, Boudreau used one of his regular pitchers and told him to cut loose when Howe came to plate.

Gordie drove the third pitch into the leftfield seats.

Howe has always been a man of modesty. He never considered himself more than a working man.

And he always had others in his mind. How many times readers would write letters to the newspapers praising Howe for his humanity — how he'd stop his car in the middle of a snowstorm and help some guy dig out his driveway or, at last minute, show up at a boy scout meeting when some ball player failed to make it.

When Ned Harkness — not a popular man — took over the Red Wings' management, the media went right after him because he was an outsider. They kept badgering him, asking if he anticipated any problems from the older players since he was an outsider and no one from the organization got the job.

The question caught Harkness by surprise. Would he have trouble with the older players? As he prepared to answer, a voice from the back of the room was heard. Just one word: "No!"

It was, of course, Gordie Howe.

At an All-Star game, Bobby Baun, defenseman of the hated Toronto Maple Leafs came into the dressing room. He was sweating profusely and his uniform was wet. He slumped in front of his locker, too exhausted to go any further.

Howe walked by. He handed Baun a Coke bottle which he'd just filled with cold water. And out the door he went, without a word passing between either man.

Baun drank thirstily and shook his head and smiled.

Howe played so long he outlasted six U.S. Presidents and five Canadian prime ministers. But he never lost his humility or humanity.

How many times the Red Wings' bus was late leaving for the arena or coming home from the arena because Howe was standing on the sidewalk signing autographs for everyone? And every time he signed he said: "Thank you."

He was on the laconic side and on the nights he was tired, it merely seemed like a reflection of his personality. The truth is, he was tired, or feeling sick — even fevered at times.

Some nights he would have trouble holding his head up. Nobody thought much of it because this was the great Gordie Howe, a man of iron. Somewhere along the way, he would summon up enough strength of make a play no one else could even dream about and his team would squeeze through to victory.

On the nights he was feeling strong — and that was most nights — he would simply take over the games.

As Bobby Hull once said: "Tonight we play Toronto, tomorrow night Boston and Gordie Howe on Sunday."

Howe's performances would all but defy description. He would turn this way, then that way, deking one player, slamming into another, chasing the puck into the corner, muscling his way in front of the net, forechecking, backchecking, passing, shooting

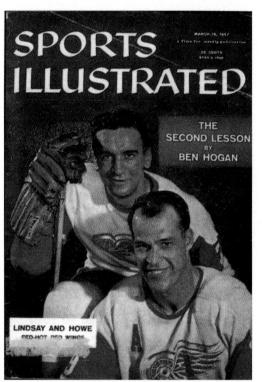

and controlling the entire ice. He was a complete team player, never caring much for personal statistics.

Nobody ever kept count but he passed up countless goals when he would pass the puck to a teammate. A personal opinion is that if Howe had the demonic drive for scoringgoals as did Maurice Richard, they would still be chas-

ing his records to this day.

But then, he wouldn't have been Gordie Howe, the Gentle Giant. His strength was awesome.

Alex Delvecchio remembers a particular goal against the New York Rangers.

"I fired the puck in and it went off Gordie's pants right past goalie Jacques Plante," said Delvecchio. "It seemed like an accident but it wasn't. He was always battling in front of the net and winning most of the battles. This time three guys were trying to muscle him out of there, but, when he saw the puck coming, he stuck his butt out and deflected the puck into the net. He'd get nine or 10 goals a season just by roughhousing it in front of the goalie."

Howe was a wrist shooter. The slap shot had not yet really taken over the game.

One day, in practice, he said to a newsman: "Where do you want this puck to go?"

He was 25 feet from the net.

"Left goal post," said the newsman.

Clang! The puck rang off the left goal post.

"Next?" said Howe.

"Right goal post," said the newsman.

Clang! You guessed it.

Howe was the only ambidextrous shooter in the league. His strength was that he could hold

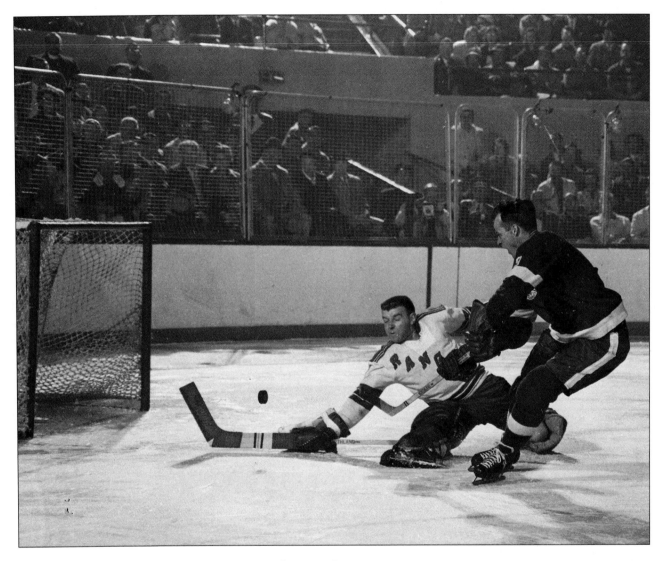

In this duel with a New York Rangers goalie, Gordie Howe came out a winner.

off defender with one hand and shoot with the other hand.

Howe might hurt you with his body but never with his words.

When he showed up on the day before they began tearing down Olympia Stadium, a woman who had worked in the building stood in the darkness of the old place and said to Howe: "I feel awful. This whole place doesn't look the same."

Gordie replied: "None of us do."

Art Skov, the old referee, showed up for one last look at the Red Barn.

With Howe watching from the side where the Red Wings' bench used to be, Skov cried out: "That's it, Howe! Two minutes! High sticking! You're out of here!"

As the tour was winding up, Howe called one of the construction workers aside and whispered to him. He asked: "Could you go up into the balcony and get the penalty clock for me?"

Just an old softie.

RED WINGS COME HOME FOR THE 'KILL'

Flames Heat Up, But Detroit Extinguishes Rival

By Vartan Kupelian

The Detroit News

After the playoff pressure, heat and humidity had suffocated even the most casual observer last night in the Omni, Wings coach Bobby Kromm coolly dismissed the Atlanta Flames' third-period rally.

"They aren't that great a club that they can overcome four goals," Kromm said.

The Flames certainly tried, however.

The Wings "powered" their way to a 4-0 first-period lead and then held on to extinguish the Flames, 5-3, in the opening game of their Stanley Cup playoff preliminary series.

The teams meet again tomorrow night in Detroit's Olympia in the second game of the best-of-three series, and the Wings are hoping it's also the last.

Detroit scored three power-play goals in a span of 2 minutes 40 seconds of the first period — by Dale McCourt, Errol Thompson and Vaclav Nedomansky. Captain Den-

RED WINGS

5

FLAMES

3

Atlanta,
April 11, 1978

nis Hextall, continuing his hot scoring streak, added a shorthanded goal before the period ended. He has scored in each of the last five games.

The Wings didn't score again until Andre St. Laurent slid the puck into an empty net with one second left in the game.

In between the Detroit scoring, someone lit the Flames and they responded with goals by Guy Chouinard, Eric Vail and Dick Redmond. Vail's goal came at the nine-second mark of the third period, and when Redmond scored at 8:07 it was anybody's hockey game.

With about eight minutes left, the Wings — badly outplayed in the previous 30 minutes and resembling a punch-drunk fighter on the ropes waiting to by KO'd — somehow summoned a reserve and played much, much better.

"That third period was the way we should have been playing all along after we got the lead," Kromm said.

"Seven out of 10 times when you have such a big lead so early, the oth-

er team comes back, especially if it's the home team that's down," said Nick Libett. "You just have a natural tendency to relax. You don't like to do it, but it happens just the same.

"It's a super feeling to be going back to Detroit knowing all we need is a victory at home. We had to win a game down here, and we did. Now it's up to us to get them again on Thursday."

The Wings had been labeled the underdog in this best two-of-three-game series because of Atlanta's superior regular-season record, its home-ice advantage and season-ending hot streak.

"I like being the underdog," Kromm said. "I've always liked it. It's something to sell the players. Personally, I didn't think we were."

They certainly aren't now.

"Now they have to come to our building, and we'll definitely play differently at home," Kromm said. "Atlanta tried to play a different game than they have all season, and it hurt them.

"They went out to intimidate us, and they paid the price. It cost them the game. They've been getting a lot of press, saying they're a big, tough club, even though

The 1977-78 Red Wings made the playoffs for the first time in eight seasons.

they haven't played that way."

The Flames took some curious penalties in the first period, and that's when the Wings won the game.

Harold Phillipoff, the huge (6-foot-4) Atlanta rookie, cross-checked Detroit's mild-mannered McCourt. That was followed by roughing penalties to Dennis Polonich and Greg Fox — who played his college hockey at the University of Michigan — with Fox in the role of aggressor. The Wings enjoyed a 4-on-3 advantage for 56 seconds, but they didn't need that much time.

McCourt opened the scoring at 4:52 during that power play, with Nedomansky and Libett assisting.

Atlanta defenseman Dave Shand took a senseless penalty when he cross-checked Libett, breaking his stick in half against the Detroit veteran's arm. Bill Clement followed him off the ice

for hooking Thompson — it was either that or let him in on the net alone.

The Wings wasted little time in their two-man advantage, with Thompson converting Nedomansky's pass at 7:05. Just 27 seconds later, with Clement still in the penalty box, Nedomansky intercepted a passout right on the blue line, took one stride and blazed a high shot past Atlanta goalie Dan Bouchard, who didn't give the Flames the big game they were looking for.

"It should just have been an ordinary shoulder check," Libett said. "Like a dummy, he (Shand) comes in with a full two-hander. It caused them to lose the game. I've had a lot harder checks than that thrown at me."

Hextall finished off the first-period scoring at 15:18 while killing off a penalty to Jean Hamel. Hextall blocked a shot at his own blue line,

outraced the defense and went in alone on Bouchard, who raced a good 20 feet out of his net, allowing Hextall to easily go around him.

Naturally, the Wings are looking for a sweep.

"It was tough enough tonight with this heat and humidity," said St. Laurent. "We don't want to come back and have to go through it again. That's why we had some trouble in the third period. We were taking 30-second shifts. I think it hurt them, too, and it showed late in the game.

"Ronnie (Low) saved us early in the game; that was the game right there. And Jean Hamel, what a game he played."

In the second minute of play, Low robbed Clement on what looked like a sure goal. After that, the only sure thing was a victory at least in Kromm's mind.

WINGS AND FOES TO MISS THE ICE AT COZY HOME

Detroit Wraps Memorable Era at Olympia Stadium

By Vartan Kupelian

The Detroit News

Right down to the bad visitors bench, Olympia Stadium was perfect for the home team.

When the ice was good, which was most of the time, it was the best in the National Hockey League. When it was bad, it slipped a notch to second best.

Will the Red Wings miss Olympia and its hard and fast ice surface? Will they miss the coziness of the corners and those weird ricochets off the boards?

"They sure will," said Harry Neale, coach of the Vancouver Canucks. "They're going to miss this rink."

The Wings played their final game Saturday night in the Olympia against the Quebec Nordiques, which concluded in a 4-4 tie. They're scheduled to be in their new home, the Joe Louis Arena on the riverfront, for the Dec. 27 game against the St. Louis Blues. The ice surface will be laid down on the

NORDIQUES

4

RED WINGS

4

Detroit,
Dec. 15, 1979

floor of the Louis Arena next Saturday to allow it time to cure.

"Olympia is a tough place to come and play," Neale said. "If the fans get excited and start making all that noise, it's hard on a visiting team. It looks like they're right on top of you. It won't be like that in the new building.

"This (Olympia) is the kind of rink you can get to know. It has characteristics you can take advantage of, the way the puck comes off the boards. They have lively boards here and that can be tough, especially on a goalie who isn't familiar with them."

Neale, as coach of the World Hockey Association's Minnesota Fighting Saints, was involved in a midseason shift of arenas a few years ago.

"It was a tough adjustment," he said. "It takes time to get the feel of a new rink. Besides, they've got great ice at Olympia."

Neale added that there were other advantages at Olympia for the home team that won't exist in the

new 19,500-seat Joe Louis Arena.

"The visitors' bench is bad here and so is the dressing room," he said.

Coach Bobby Kromm shrugged off the switch.

"Hopefully, there won't be a problem," he said. "I suppose there has to be some period of adjustment.

"They all say that most teams come in here and play their best hockey because they like the ice and the building so much. The Montreal Canadiens say they love to come here because it's the best ice in the circuit. Maybe if the new building has poor ice, it'll be to our advantage.

"I don't care what the ice is like as long as we win them all."

It's not likely that soft and sloppy ice will be to Detroit's advantage. The Red Wings are a skating club and when they go into a foreign building and the ice isn't fast and hard, it's a cause for concern. It takes away their speed, and speed is their game.

A look at the Wings' performances over he past two decades show conclusively that the club is

In their last 10 seasons at Olympia Stadium, the Red Wings won 173 games.

far superior at Olympia than it is on the road.

In the last 10 seasons, dating back to 1969-70, the Wings have won 173 games at home and 93 on the road. In the decade before that, from 1959-60 to 1968-69, when the club was far more successful than it has been in the last 10 years, the Wings won more than two-thirds of all their games on home ice, 199 victories against 95 losses.

It's true that the home team owns an advantage in any building, but the Wings' performance chart is particularly one-sided. For instance, in the last 10 seasons, the Rangers have 221 games at home and 166 on the road. The Boston Bruins have won 285 games at home, 200 on the road.

The Los Angeles Kings, one of the original expansion teams, have won 188 at home and 114 on the road.

Of course, the opposite could be true. Maybe now the Wings, having one of their own, will feel more comfortable in those new arenas around the league and improve their performances in them.

NEW ERA, BUT WINGS OLD HAT

19,742 See Opener at Joe Louis Arena

By Vartan Kupelian

The Detroit News

The sightlines are dandy, and there aren't any posts to block the view. The corners are shaped a little differently, but so what? No one goes there anyway.

The Joe Louis Arena passed its first hockey test as the new home of the Detroit Red Wings last night. It was the Wings who flunked.

The Wings' debut in the new building — a 3-2 loss to the St. Louis Blues before a record Detroit hockey crowd of 19,742 — was not unlike another more than half a century ago. In that one, the Wings lost their first game at Olympia 52 years ago, 2-1, to the old Ottawa Senators. They went on from that defeat to become one of the great teams in the National Hockey League.

Now the Wings are near the bottom in the NHL, and hoping for a renaissance — just like the city they represent.

BLUES

3

RED WINGS

2

Detroit,
Dec. 27, 1979

"I thought tonight we could start a new era ... not that we still can't ... but we certainly have to start (doing it) soon," said Bobby Kromm, the coach of the Red Wings.

St. Louis rallied for the victory with third-period goals by Bernie Federko and Blair Chapman. The Wings led, 2-1, entering the final period. Brian Sutter, the Blues' captain, scored the first goal in the arena at 11:05 of the first period with Federko drawing the lone assist.

The first Detroit goal was scored by Dennis Sobchuk at 1:43 of the second period. Danny Bolduc added another goal as the Wings dominated the Blues in the second period, but let them off the hook.

The crowd, which surpassed the previous Detroit hockey high of 16,678 at Olympia on Nov. 1, 1978, against the Montreal Canadiens, included numerous standees. Once the arena is completed — the private boxes ringing the arena and 204 executive seats remain unfinished

— the seating capacity for hockey will by 19,442. At that figure, plus standing room, the NHL attendance record of 20,009 set in St. Louis in 1973, is certain to fall.

Instead of a new hockey club for the new building the fans saw the same old Red Wings, a team that now ranks 17th among the 21 NHL teams. The loss was Detroit's third straight and the Wings have a 1-6-2 record in their last nine games. The Blues aren't much better — they presently rank 16th, the final playoff spot — but on this night they were good enough.

After a ceremonial faceoff at center ice with NHL President John Ziegler and Senator Carl Levin doing the honors, the game started 15 minutes late. It took the Wings a good while longer to get started. It should be noted that the first cheer went to referee Bruce Hood, who fell after dropping the first puck.

"When your two big lines don't do anything, then you don't have anything going," Kromm said.

"It didn't really seem like a home game. It felt strange. We had

---

The Red Wings abandoned their 52-year-old home on Grand River for the new Joe Louis Arena.

good ice at Olympia. This was soft ... shavings. It's more of a disadvantage to us."

Federko tied the score at 11:16 of the final period. Detroit defenseman Barry Long was penalized for interference at 13:15, and Chapman scored the winning goal 26 seconds later.

Goalie Rogie Vachon appeared to have the puck beneath him on Chapman's goal.

"That guy behind the net (Federko) surprised me," Vachon said. "I came across the net and tired to reach it with my stick. The other guy (Chapman) hit it first, and it went through my legs."

Coach Red Berenson of the Blues said, "It was one of those games where we got the breaks, being able to hold them off when we were shorthanded and then scoring on our power play."

Berenson, a former Red Wing, complimented the new building.

"Everything worked," he said. "Usually in a new arena, the glass falls or the scoreboard doesn't work."

Only the numbers of the scoreboard spoiled the occasion: VISITORS 3, HOME 2.

NHL RECORD FALLS AS 21,019 CHEER WINGS TO VICTORY

Eddie Mio Wins Duel of Goalies

By Vartan Kupelian

The Detroit News

A record deserves the proper finishing touches, and the Detroit Red Wings were equal to the occasion last night.

The Wings treated a Joe Louis Arena crowd of 21,019 — the largest ever for a National Hockey League game — to a 5-2 victory over the Pittsburgh Penquins.

The Wings got goals from Ivan Boldirev, Ron Duguay and rookies Steve Yzerman, Lane Lambert (his first in the NHL) and Kelly Kisio to register their ninth victory of the season. They needed 39 games, or just one game less than half a season, to win nine game last season.

All the news wasn't good, however, for the Wings. Right winger Ed Johnstone suffered a depressed fracture of the right cheekbone in a third-period collision with teammate Dwight Foster. He underwent surgery last night at the Detroit Osteopathic Hospital.

With Johnstone joining Danny Gare, already sidelined with a chest injury, on the sidelines, the Wings needed immediate replacements.

PENGUINS

2

RED WINGS

5

Detroit,
Nov. 25, 1983

Coach Nick Polano and General Manager Jim Devellano huddled after the game, and later telephoned Bill Dineen, coach of Detroit's top farm club in Glens Falls, N.Y., to send left winger Joe Paterson and right wingers Brad Smith to the Wings.

The crowd falls into the "Only in Detroit" category. It was amazing, even if there were some 2,000 complimentary tickets included in the attendance figure. Besides, many of those, if not all, probably would have been sold to the standees who engulfed the arena.

"That was unreal," said Yzerman, who scored his 14th goal. "When we came out for the warmup and looked up, we knew it was going to be big. A lot of times in front of a big crowd like that, you play nervous. But the guys went out and played well. It was an exciting game."

The previous NHL record crowd of 21,002, also at Joe Louis, attended the 1980 All-Star game.

Of course, the setting was almost perfect — a holiday weekend and a jersey giveaway. Almost perfect.

On the other side of the ledger was the fact that the Penquins, not Wayne Gretzky and the Edmonton Oilers or the NHL All-Stars, provided the opposition.

The Penquins are a nondescript collection of hockey players named McSorley, Buskas, Tebbutt, Errey and Hotham, hardly household names even in Pittsburgh where they have averaged about 8,100 fans a game this season.

But the Penquins have a goalie who is enjoying an exceptional season. Denis Herron leads the NHL with a 2.45 goals-against average and a .925 save percentage, allowing just 27 goals on 363 shots. Except for Herron, the

Ron Duguay was one of five Red Wings to score a goal against Pittsburgh.

Wings might have beaten the Penquins as bad as the Lions carved up the Steelers a day earlier. Herron faced 39 shots.

Red Wing goalie Eddie Mio stopped 29 shots in posting his second straight victory. Rick Kehoe and Rob Flockhart scored for Pittsburgh.

The teams will do it all over again tonight in a rematch in Pittsburgh. Minus the crowd, of course.

The Wings outshot Pittsburgh, 15-7 in the opening period. But Detroit's power play was balky and Herron was outstanding in goal for the Penquins.

The Wings killed off an early penalty to Greg Smith. Moments later, Herron stopped Yzerman on a breakaway and Duguay on the ensuing rebound.

Boldirev opened the scoring at 11:40 with an assisted goal. He picked off a loose puck just outside the faceoff circle to Herron's right and fired a shot in off the Pittsburgh goalie.

The Penquins have resorted to a clutching, holding style and they have paid for it— they are the third most penalized team in the NHL — but the Wings couldn't capitalize on three power-play opportunities in the first period.

FIVE GOALS IN THIRD PERIOD TURN TABLES ON LEAFS

John Ogrodnick Scores Third-Period Hat Trick

By Vartan Kupelian

The Detroit News

It was bizarre.

For two periods last night, the Red Wings lived a nightmare.

"Then we woke up," Reed Larson said.

Just in time to see the Toronto Maple Leafs fall into a trance of their own and blow a 6-2 lead.

With John Ogrodnick scoring 3 goals in a 5-goal, third period explosion, the Red Wings KO'd the Leafs 7-6 at Joe Louis Arena.

Even though the NHL season is still only a couple of months old, it was a critical contest for a couple of faltering team who entered the game residing near the bottom of the overall standings — the Wings were 19th, the Leafs 20th among the 21 teams. The Wings were coming off a disastrous weekend in which they lost twice to St. Louis, a Norris Division rival like Toronto. And the Leafs had only one victory in 17 previous games.

MAPLE LEAFS

6

RED WINGS

7

Detroit,
Dec. 4, 1984

And that's just about how they played. First the Wings tried to give it away. They didn't succeed even at that. Then the Leafs tried to give it away. And finally did.

Ogrodnick started his fifth career hat trick at 5:18 of the final period and ended it at 19:11 with the winning goal.

The Wings, trailing by 4 goals entering the final period, got goals from Ogrodnick, Frank Cernik and Steve Yzerman to close to within a goal.

Ogrodnick tied it at 14:17 before winning it with his 14th goal of the season. Both goals came on his big slap shot.

"It was the quietest I've ever heard this room after two periods," Ogrodnick said of the Wings' dressing quarters.

"It (the comeback) couldn't have happened at a better time. Nick (Polano) was positive, he said to keep our heads up, that we could do it."

No doubt. The Leafs give up goals by the bundle — only once in the past 17 games have they given up fewer than 4 goals in a game.

"I've been in games like this before," said veteran Wing defenseman Colin Campbell, who has been on the receiving end on a couple of occasions.

"Once it gets to 6-4, it starts rolling on you."

Ogrodnick agreed that Cernik's goal, at 6:27, was the key.

"I got the third goal, but Frank's goal was the big one," said Ogrodnick, who posted a 4-point night with an assist on Yzerman's goal. "It's the one that got us going."

Ogrodnick (his first) and Yzerman scored on power plays, with the Yzerman goal coming while the Wings were playing four men to three in front of the goaltenders. The situation resulted from a 5-minute major for high-sticking assessed against Wing goaltender Greg Stefan and a minor against Toronto's Walt Poddubny for interference in the crease.

Before Poddubny could return to give the Leafs a power play. Ref-

---

eree Terry Greggson gave the Wings the edge by penalizing Borje Salming. That's when Yzerman scored.

The Wings killed off the rest of the major penalty and, moments later, Ogrodnick fired a shot from the blue line past Toronto goaltender Ken Wregget to tie it.

Brad Park and Lane Lambert also scored for the Wings.

Miroslav Frycer scored twice for the Leafs, with Russ Courtnall, Stewart Gavin, Salming and Bill Derlago also beating Stefan.

"Once you start letting John Ogrodnick shoot the puck from where he wants to shoot it, he's going to score," said Dan Maloney, the rookie Toronto coach who received a pregame vote of confidence from owner Harold Ballard.

"We played two periods the way we should and then stopped.

"It should have never happen. Never."

The Red Wings take their 0-10-1 road record to Toronto for a rematch tonight but, coming off such a high, the chances of finally winning on the road appear excellent.

In the first two periods the Wings made the Leafs, who had

John Ogrodnick's hat trick came in the Wings' five-goal scoring spree.

scored only 72 goals — a goal shy of the worst output in the NHL — look like an offensive machine to equal the Stanley Cup champion Edmonton Oilers.

For example: Courtnall, a rookie who has scored 2 goals in 22 games this season against the rest of the NHL, notched his fourth in three games against Detroit to give the Leafs a 1-0 lead at 2:04.

Gavin, who has scored 1 goal in 22 games against all other opposition, scored his second goal in three

games against the Wings at 3:20 as he roamed at will in the Detroit end before beating Stefan.

Salming, the veteran defenseman, scored his second goal of the season on a power play at 7:37 for a 3-0 lead before the game was 8 minutes old.

But all was not lost. After all, the Leafs are 20th goals against with a 4.67 mark.

So it was inevitable that the Wings were going to get back in the game, and they did.

DETROIT BOMBARDS BLACKHAWKS, 12-0

A Potpourri of Red Wings in Scoring Spree

By Cynthia Lambert

The Detroit News

A dictionary wasn't necessary.

The Red Wings definition of "rout" was clear Friday night when they pounded the Chicago Blackhawks 12-0 at Joe Louis Arena.

It was the fifth consecutive victory for the Wings and fifth consecutive loss for the Blackhawks.

Detroit continued to showcase its newfound offense, scoring six goals in the first period, three in the second and three in the third.

Helping matters was an almost non-existent Chicago defense — not to mention goaltending and offense. In other words, the Blackhawks played with all the interest of millionaires at a garage sale.

"It was unbelievable," said John Chabot, who contributed two assists to the effort. "Unbelievable is the only way I can describe it.

BLACKHAWKS

0

RED WINGS

12

Detroit,
Dec. 4, 1987

We didn't even really force the issue after six, seven or eight goals. I can't even remember when that point actually came. How many goals did we have at the end of the first period?"

Six.

The first two were scored in the opening minute — the first by Tim Higgins and the second by Steve Yzerman. Before the period ended, Higgins had scored again. Joe Murphy, Petr Klima and Brent Ashton added the finishing touches to a 6-0 lead.

Despite the score, Chicago coach Bob Murdoch kept starter Bob Mason in goal. But that last only another period, as the Wings, again, peppered Mason with 16 shots.

After Bob Probert scored to make it 7-0, Higgins scored on a pass from Jeff Sharples, achieving his first career hat trick. Before the period ended, Yzerman would score again to make it, 9-0.

All the while, Wings goaltender Greg Stefan kept himself amused at the other end of the ice, gathering ice shavings with his stick and flinging them into the net. They were the only things that entered the Detroit net Friday, as Stefan gained his fifth career shutout — third against Chicago.

But by the time the third period began, Mason was sitting on the bench.

Exit Mason. Enter Darren Pang.

Joe Kocur, Gerald Gallant and Klima each scored in the third, giving the Wings their gaudy total.

It was the second-most lopsided victory in the history of the Red Wings franchise. On Jan. 23, 1944, the Wings defeated the New York Rangers, 15-0.

"I know I wanted us to score more goals," Wings coach Jacques Demers said. "But 10? Then 12? No coach in his right mind would expect that from his team. There was no way I could predict this team would score that many goals."

Last week the Wings scored

10 goals to defeat the Winnipeg Jets. Until Friday night, that was Detroit's biggest offensive output.

After reflecting on that, Demers confessed: "This is a happy coach sitting right here. But I can't get too excited and let the guys know it. We've got such a young team and we can't carried away with a game like this. I want them to have fun with this. That's what winning's all about. But I can't let it go to their heads.

"But I admit, I am a very excited coach. You know what I have right now? Right now, I have an awesome team."

Murdoch has a team in shambles.

"It could have been worse," Murdoch said. "They could have scored 15 goals.

"In the first minute, we were down by two goals. They got excited. They started scoring at will and we sat back. Maybe it's time we got blown out this badly. The goaltenders have been keeping it close. If the goaltenders hadn't been standing on their heads in other games, they (the opposition) would have scored 10 or 12 goals."

Detroit goalie Greg Stefan got his fifth career shutout — and third against Chicago — in the Red Wings' 12-0 win.

KNEE INJURY SHELVES WINGS' STAR IN WIN

Team Scrambling with Yzerman Out for Season

By Cynthia Lambert

The Detroit News

The worst thing that could possibly happen to the Red Wings happened Tuesday night. Although they defeated the Buffalo Sabres, 4-0, the Red Wings lost the services of All-Star center and captain Steve Yzerman for the rest of the regular season and the playoffs with a knee injury.

SABRES

0

RED WINGS

4

Detroit,
March 1, 1988

With 1:59 left to play in the second period, Yzerman cut in on Sabres goaltender Tom Barrasso. Buffalo defenseman Calle Johansson stopped Yzerman's progress with a clean check, sending Yzerman sliding across the ice toward the goal. Yzerman stopped by crashing his right knee into the goal post, knocking the net off its magnets. Yzerman attempted to get up, but instead fell to the ice, writhing in pain.

After being assisted off the ice by

Steve Yzerman battles with a Sabres defender for position.

Wings physical therapist Jim Pengelly and teammate Doug Halward. Yzerman was taken to Detroit's Hutzel Hospital for an examination by Wings physician Dr. Robert Teitge. A preliminary diagnosis showed Yzerman has a severe strain of the posterior cruciate ligament, which connects the knee to the top of the calf.

Surgery was tentatively scheduled for today but could be postponed

so the Wings can receive a second opinion.

But one thing won't change. Yzerman is out for the season.

"It's a tremendous tragedy to lose Stevie," said an emotional Jacques Demers. "Stevie's our franchise. Not to take anything away from any of the other players, but Stevie has taken us to where we are now.

"I have to be honest with you.

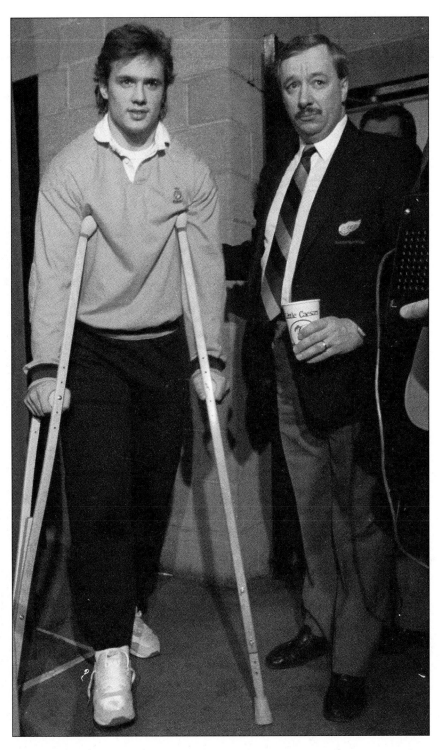

Red Wings coach Jacques Demers and his injured star after the game.

Before each game I pray that Stevie doesn't get hurt. The way he rushes to the net every night and cuts in toward the goal, you just have to hope that nothing like this ever happens."

But it did. And Demers, like several of the players, remember their reaction when they saw Yzerman bounce off the net and then painfully pound the ice with his left skate.

"I felt like I was shot," Demers said, staring ahead at the wall. "I felt like that and I'm sure the assistant coaches felt like that, and the players, too. I actually felt like someone shot me. I got all numb. I'm still numb. But I knew when he didn't get up, he was done. I knew it. I just knew it."

Getting lost in the shuffle was that Yzerman, at the beginning of the second period, gave the Wings a 2-0 lead with his 50th goal of the season — one of the few personal goals Yzerman would admit to wanting.

"God, at least he got his 50th," said Yzerman's close friend and teammate Gerald Gallant, who will replace Yzerman as team captain for the remainder of the season. "That would have been just awful if he hadn't scored his 50th. Just awful."

That goal, plus an assist, gave Yzerman a team-leading 102 points for the season. Gallant is second, with 28 goals and 34 assists for 62 points.

Also scoring for the Wings, who snapped a four-game losing streak with the victory, were Darren Veitch, Halward and Gallant.

YZERMAN'S SLICK; OILERS CHIPPED

Captain Scores Two Goals; Season Total at 63

By Cynthia Lambert

The Detroit News

Steve Yzerman did it again.

But it wasn't just his first-ever NHL six-point performance, which led the Red Wings to a 8-6 victory over the Stanley Cup champion Edmonton Oilers that dumbfounded his teammates and opponents Wednesday night.

It was his perfectly executed chip shot over Oilers defenseman Kevin Lowe, which resulted in his second goal of the game and gave Detroit its final goal with 21 seconds to play.

With Detroit leading, 7-6, and 53 seconds left to play, Oilers replacement goaltender Grant Fuhr left the net for the extra attacker. Gerald Gallant flipped the puck to Yzerman, who popped the puck over Lowe.

And as the puck tumbled into the empty net, the Red Wings players on the bench chucked.

RED WINGS

8

OILERS

6

Edmonton,
March 15, 1989

"How did he do that?" asked Wings forward Tim Higgins. "The guy (Lowe) was going to block the shot, so Stevie just made a chip shot over him. The guy was right in front of him. I don't know how Stevie did that. Incredible."

"I was right behind him, I knew what he was going to try and do," said Oilers center Jimmy Carson, a Grosse Pointe Woods native, who also scored two goals Wednesday. "I knew what he was thinking. He didn't want to take the shot, because it would just hit Kevin. So he popped it up. That's something you try at practice; I know I do. But I've never done it in a game. Not like that."

In typical Yzerman fashion, the Wings captain played down the goal after the game. "I didn't want to blast it because he was right there," he said. "My main concern was to get it in deep. I just flipped it up in the air. It was a sigh of

relief that it went in. If it doesn't, who knows? They could come back and score and tie it up."

As Yzerman, who now has 63 goals and 146 points, was swarmed by reporters in the visitors dressing room at the Northlands Coliseum, defenseman Lee Norwood and right wing Joe Kocur sat across the room on a bench and watched the scene.

"Hey, I got an assist," Norwood said.

"I did, too," Kocur added.

With that, the two smiled at each other, shook hands and turned their attention back to the scene across the room.

"It was a very nice approach shot," Norwood said, mimicking a TV golf commentator.

"That's an eagle for sure," Kocur added.

Regardless of the interpretation, it was the finishing touch on a wild game that touched on every facet of hockey.

In the first period, there was tight checking by both sides. Still, the Wings took a 2-0 lead into the

---

second period on goals by Yzerman and Torri Robertson — his first as a Red Wing.

That's when the wide-open style began. By the end of the second period, the Wings held a 5-4 lead, thanks to goals by Steve Chiasson, Gallant (power play) and Shawn Burr.

Former Michigan State standout Craig Simpson scored twice for Edmonton in the period, and Craig Muni and Carson accounted for the others.

When the third period began, the Oilers changed goalie, removing Bill Ranford from the net and replacing him with the experienced Fuhr.

Jari Kurri and Carson sandwiched goals around a short-handed goal by Detroit's John Chabot by 12:02 of the third to create a 6-6 tie.

But Paul MacLean tipped in an Yzerman pass at 18:31 to give the Wings the 7-6 lead and set up Yzerman's unique empty-net goal.

"That chip shot at the end of the game was the icing on the cake," Wings coach Jacques Demers said. "I don't know if he used a nine-iron or what. But that's Steve. He keeps on doing those things."

In typical Steve Yzerman fashion, he played down his nifty second goal against Edmonton.

YZERMAN GIVES OILERS FOUR-GOAL THRASHING

Wings Captain 'Virtually Unstoppable' in Comeback Victory

By Cynthia Lambert

The Detroit News

It was an exciting night for Steve Yzerman.

How exciting?

■ Yzerman had his first-ever four-goal game.

■ He left the ice after being cut on the leg, but returned to lead Detroit's comeback in a 7-5 victory over the Edmonton Oilers.

■ And if that weren't excitement enough, Yzerman, a big baseball fan, schmoozed afterward with Tigers baseball heroes, Alan Trammell and Jack Morris.

Steve Yzerman a star-struck superstar? Evidently.

The post-game appearance by Trammell and Morris brought a non-stop grin to Yzerman's face and caused a bit of a stir in the Wings' dressing room, but it was nothing compared to the commotion caused by the Wings' comeback.

"I was just very excited tonight," said Yzerman, who has 39 goals this

OILERS
5

RED WINGS
7

Detroit,
Jan. 31, 1990

season. "We were all excited. The whole team played with excitement. I don't know if it was the crowd and the way they got behind us. It seemed everyone tonight had a lot of emotion."

That emotion was particularly evident after Yzerman's third goal. The Wings' captain typically raises his stick almost meekly after scoring but on this goal he leaped up and punched the air in atypical exuberance.

"I think it was a kind of a mixture of things," said Yzerman, who also had an assist as Detroit won the three-game season series from the Oilers, two games to one. "We're running out of games, and we're playing one of the best teams in the league ... There was a sense of urgency. We haven't shown a lot of emotion lately. I think that was the most encouraging thing out of this."

Yzerman also had to be encouraged by the way the Wings rallied from a 4-3 deficit his brief absence early in the third.

Yzerman cut his left leg when he

brushed against the blade of Oilers goaltender Bill Ranford's skate.

"It was only three or four stitches," Yzerman said. But it was enough to sideline him for several minutes.

No matter. Goals by Joe Kocur and Bernie Federko made it 5-4. Yzerman's third goal made it 6-4. Edmonton picked up a two-man advantage with less than seven minutes left when Yzerman was called for interfering with Ranford. On the delayed penalty, Rick Zombo was whistled for cross-checking Craig Simpson in front of the Wings net at 13:30.

But Glen Hanlon made three saves — one on Mark Messier, two on Esa Tikkanen — to help preserve the lead. Defenseman Lee Norwood did his part as well, stopping a Jari Kurri slap shot that left a impression of a puck on his stomach.

"Jari, is that who it was?" Norwood said. "That sounds right. It sure knocked the wind out of me."

The Wings also deflated the Oilers' power play (0-for-7) Wednesday night. Going into the game, Edmonton's power play was ranked ninth in the league and Detroit's penalty killing was 20th.

"I was just very excited tonight," Steve Yzerman said after deflating the Oilers with four goals.

"They blocked a lot of shots and Glenny made some big, big saves," said penalty-killing specialist John Chabot. "Our defensemen really helped out. I know Lee got the one right in the gut. Stevie had a big game, too. He played outstanding. It shouldn't surprise us, we know what kind of player he is. We just have to make sure we help him."

After the Wings killed the Oilers' two-man advantage, Edmonton rallied when Steve Smith scored at 16:18 to made it 6-5. But Yzerman's fourth goal into an empty net with 50 seconds left helped the Wings (18-27-6) stay nine points behind fourth-place Minnesota in the Norris Division with 29 games to play.

Detroit took a 2-1 lead after one period on goals by Gerald Gallant and Yzerman, who added a second goal in the middle period. But scores by Simpson (two), Craig MacTavish and Vladmir Ruzicka gave Edmonton a 4-3 lead going into the third period. The Oilers are 22-1-1 when leading after two periods.

"Anytime we lead going into the third period we should protect it," said Edmonton's Adam Graves, a former Wing. "We didn't take advantage of our opportunities."

Yzerman did. That was the difference.

"Yzerman's a great player and virtually unstoppable," said Petr Klima, another former Wing. "We have to watch him a lot closer."

After 30 Years of Glory, the Red Wings Became Losers

Detroit Hits 40-Year Slump on the Ice

By Jerry Green
The Detroit News

Forty-two years later, Ted Lindsay remains burned up. He is volatile, explosive, angered at the destruction of a dynasty.

"It was the dumbest, stupidest thing that ever happened to the Red Wings," he said in the old Lindsay fashion. "We had a dynasty. We won the championship. The only place we had a weakness at that time was on defense."

Lindsay was speaking just after the Red Wings had broken their 42-year curse. It was August 1997, and another generation of Red Wings had won the Stanley Cup in a four-game sweep of the Philadelphia Flyers. Captain Steve Yzerman circled the rink at Joe Louis Arena pumping the Cup upward to the shrieks of the hockey fans.

Earlier on this June Saturday night, Lindsay had been given a rousing ovation by the long-deprived when his scarred mug appeared on the graphic board above the ice.

Flashback. Forty-two years earlier, in 1955, he was captain when the Red Wings won the Stanley Cup at Olympia Stadium – their fourth ultimate ice-hockey championship in six seasons. A true dynasty. They defeated the Montreal Canadiens in seven bitter games.

Then Jack Adams broke up the Red Wings with a glut of curious trades.

He dealt away seven of the players who had just won the Cup.

Among them was Terry Sawchuk, traded to the Boston Bruins. Sawchuk, the supreme goalkeeper, had recorded four shutouts when the Red Wings won the Cup in the eight-game minimum in 1952. At age 25, Sawchuk had already won the Stanley Cup three times.

"We weren't that bad on defense,"

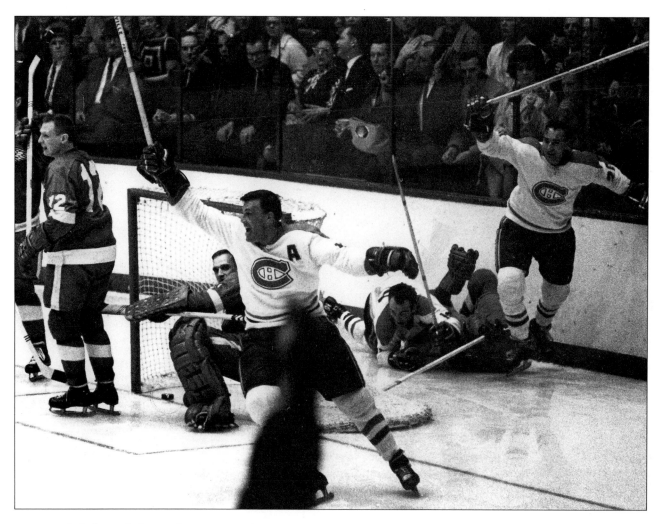

Montreal defeated the Red Wings in the Stanley Cup Finals in 1966.

Lindsay went on 42 years later. "Bob Goldham was getting old. If we'd gotten hold of Tom Johnson in a trade we'd have won the five Stanley Cup championships that Montreal won."

The Canadiens needed a goaltender and coveted Sawchuk.

"Glenn Hall was coming up," Lindsay said. Hall had been stuck in the Red Wings' farm system. He was younger, less expensive and less temperamental than Sawchuk. And maybe as skillful.

But Adams rejected the Canadiens' offer of Johnson for Sawchuk.

"Adams didn't want to make Montreal too strong," said Lindsay. "And if we could have gotten Doug Harvey, we'd have won eight more Stanley Cups."

Instead Adams traded Sawchuk to Boston.

"Our best player at the time was Vic Stasiuk," Linsday said. "Vic was ready. He was traded to Boston with Sawchuk for five players. They had never won anything . . .

"We had a line of Marty Pavelich, Glen Skov and Tony Leswick. Because of them, we were a half-goal better than anybody when the game started. They were the checking line.

Marty established the standards for the defensive forward."

Adams broke up the line that was the counterbalance to Lindsay, Gordie Howe and Sid Abel — the Production Line — and Alex Delvecchio's line — the high shooters. Skov and Leswick were traded to the Chicago Black Hawks along with Johnny Wilson and Benny Woit — all Cup winners.

Adams was a stubborn man who would never forget. His Red Wings won the Stanley Cup in 1936, after the Tigers had won the World Series and the Lions had won their first NFL championships. Detroit was The City of Champions. The Tigers and Lions failed to repeat. But the Red Wings did, winning their second Stanley Cup in '37.

"That team won the Stanley Cup and we stood pat," Adams said. "Next year it was in fourth place, and two years later it didn't make the playoffs.

"Never again."

This time Adams refused to stand pat. In the Boston deal, the Red Wings received Eddie Sanford, Warren Godfrey, Norm Corcoran, Real Chevrefils and Gilles Boisvert for Sawchuk, Stasiuk and Marcel Bonin and Lorne Davis. In the Chicago trade, Jerry Toppazzini, Dave Creighton and Bucky Hollingworth joined the Red Wings. Lindsay was absolutely correct.

None of them had won anything. Nor would they.

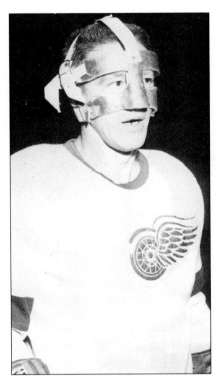

Marcel Pronovost was forced to wear this crude facemask after he broke his nose in 1955-56.

"The next guy to come up to our team," said Lindsay, "his name was John Bucyk. He'd go behind the net with his ass to the boards and get behind the play. Adams said, 'Where'd he learn to check?'"

Two years later, Adams reacquired Sawchuk. He traded Bucyk plus cash to bring Sawchuk back, igniting another batch of trades.

"Hall and I were traded to Chicago," said Lindsay. "Bucyk, he ends up playing 21 years for Boston. He played on a line with Bronco Horvath and Stasiuk. They called it the Uke Line. It was

the best line in the league."

Linsday credits not Adams but Carson Cooper, an old-time scout, for assembling the Red Wings who won the Stanley Cup in 1950, '52, '54 and '55 and finished first in the six-club NHL seven consecutive regular seasons.

"We won four Stanley Cups, and I'm very happy about that," said Lindsay. "But Henri Richard got 11 with Montreal. When I see Henri, I say, 'You got 11 Stanley Cups. Five of those are mine.'

"I say it in jest. But I'm serious, too. I don't have any vendetta against Adams. I just know what the organization was, and it bothers me. It bothers me to this day."

During the 42-year gap, the Red Wings went through the second half of the 1950's, the 1960's, 1970's, 1980's and much of the 1990's in a state of constant change and frequent chaos. They mounted few serious challenges to win the Stanley Cup again.

They traversed a period during which Jack Adams was forced into retirement after 35 years with the Detroit Hockey Club; during which the NHL expanded from the six clubs to 12 and ultimately to 26 with more in the planning; during which salaries went from a few thousand to multimillions; during which the Red Wings had 22 coaches, a couple twice, and nine general managers; during which Bruce Norris sold the franchise to pizza-maker

Toronto defeated the Red Wings in the 1963 Stanley Cup Finals.

Mike Ilitch; and during which the hockey team moved from the historic Olympia out on Grand River Avenue to Joe Louis Arena on the shore of the Detroit River.

Twelve other franchises won the Stanley Cup during the 42 years. And during that long spell of futility, Red Wings management chased the greatest player in the history of their franchise, and in the minds of Detroit fans the greatest player ever, right out of town.

Even in his farewell address Gordie Howe left them in stitches.

"I got the mushroom treatment," said Howe, as incisive with the verbal slash as he was with the sly, unseen butt end of his hockey stick. "You know what I mean — where they keep you completely in the dark and every once in a while they

come in and throw manure on you. And that's the position I've been in."

The Red Wings were keeping Howe to gawk at like an objet d'art, a priceless antique.

Those words appeared in The Detroit News on June 11, 1973, the day after the Gordie Howe Golf Tournament at Plum Hollow. Howe was the dinner speaker.

He was 45. He had played 25 seasons for the Red Wings.

Two years earlier, he had retired as a player. Rather than use his experience, his hockey wisdom, his expertise, as an advantage, the Red Wings gave him a flunkey's job as a goodwill ambassador. He sat in a small office at Olympia and twiddled.

The Mushroom Treatment.

At last, he delivered the message.

He was leaving town. He was going to the Houston Aeros in the World Hockey Association, as a player — to team with his sons, Mark and Marty. He would remain a productive player for seven more seasons with Houston and then the Hartford Whalers in the WHA and NHL before retiring as a player at age 52.

It would be three years after the 1955 Cup championship, followed by the giveaways at wholesale prices before the Red Wings' total collapse. They actually reached the Finals again in '56, but were beaten by the Canadiens.

That was the first of the five consecutive Stanley Cup championships that Lindsay believed the Red Wings might have won if they not been dumb and stupid.

Soon Jimmy Skinner, the Cup-winning coach in '55, was fired as his depleted club struggled. He was replaced by Sid Abel ("Bootnose" to his teammates), the old centerman on the Production Line with Howe and Lindsay.

The Red Wings banged to the bottom in 1958-59. They finished sixth in the six-team league. It was the first time the Detroit club had finished in last place since their very first season, back in 1926-27. It was the first time one of Jack Adams' teams had finished last.

A hasty repair job enabled the Red Wings to advance back as far as fourth place the following two seasons. And in the spring of 1961, they managed to reach the Finals again. They suffered the ignominy of losing the Stanley Cup to the Black Hawks (two words then). The Hawks had Glenn Hall in goal. Lindsay, however, had retired.

Soon after the end of the 1961-62 season, the Detroit media were summoned to Olympia. The press was ushered into the upstairs Olympia Room, with the oil paintings of nudes and lechers hanging from the walls. In this atmosphere, it was announced by Bruce Norris that Jack Adams was no longer general manager of the Detroit Hockey Club after 35 years.

Sid Abel was appointed as his successor. Old Bootnose managed to keep the Red Wings competitive as dual coach/GM, making deals, gently prodding the players. They

John Ogrodnick and the Red Wings were swept three straight in the opening round of the 1985 playoffs by Chicago.

would reach the Finals twice more — in 1964 and 1966. And each time, but for strange goings on, they might have beaten clubs superior in manpower to win the Cup.

Bill Gadsby was a tough, gnarled defenseman who'd challenge opposing players for space in front of the goalie. His face was knocked lumpy in the in-fighting. But most years he was an All-Star. And he played defense for the Wings in four successive springs in the middle 60s, when they played the Black Hawks in the Stanley Cup semifinals.

In 1964, the Wings had finished fourth among the six clubs in the regular season. They had Howe and Delvecchio, still in their prime. Gadsby, who had been with the Blackhawks and Rangers, was the leader on defense. And Sawchuk was still the goalie.

The Red Wings barely missed winning the Stanley Cup. After they'd ousted the Blackhawks in six games, they played the Maple Leafs. Detroit led Toronto, 3 games to 2, with Game 6 at Olympia.

The Red Wings had a lead, but the Leafs tied the game. In the third period, Bobby Baun, a Toronto defenseman, hobbled off the ice. He was assisted to the dressing room. It was announced that Baun's leg was broken.

Some sort of healing miracle occurred. Baun was back for the overtime.

A goal by the Red Wings would win the Stanley Cup. A goal by the Leafs would return the series to Toronto for Game 7.

Back on the ice, after his wounded leg was frozen, Baun took a routine shot from just inside the blue line. The shot seemed harmless. The puck fluttered, spun over. Then it hit something, ricocheted in an odd, sharp downward angle, bounced

and stopped in the Detroit goal behind Sawchuk.

"Baun hit my stick," Gadsby recalled. "If I hadn't put my stick up it would have hit me in the face. It might have been better.

"I didn't try to put the SOB in my net. I don't think Baun ever broke his leg. He had a crappy shot."

No Cup for Detroit.

The Leafs won Game 7 by a 4-0 score two nights later in Maple Leaf Gardens. In 1964-65, the Red Wings unexpectedly finished first in the league. They were spurred by Ted Lindsay, out of retirement at age 39, back to play a final season with his original team.

Lindsay was as fiery and pugnacious as he had been a decade earlier. He fought, he battled officials, he scored 14 goals. It was a good season.

But the Red Wings burned out in the regular season. The Blackhawks knocked them out in seven nasty games — Bobby Hull and Stan Mikita outlasting the older Howe, Lindsay and Gadsby.

The Red Wings reached the Finals one more time in the spring of 1966.

They had dropped back to fourth place again in the 1965-66 schedule, good enough for the playoffs. They beat the Blackhawks, with blood flowing, in the semis.

The Wings had obtained Bryan Watson, known as Buggsy to his teammates.

He was a journeyman defenseman with a tough streak. Coach Abel assigned Watson to the singular duty of shadowing Hull in the playoffs. Hull, then the top goal-getter in the history of hockey, was limited to two goals.

Watson matched Hull with two of his own, equalling his total for the 70-game season. Time and again Watson did whatever he was supposed to do against Hull. Hull, in frustration, retaliated. Watson's grinning face was belted lopsided from Hull's stick.

Billy Reay, the snarling little Chicago coach, would become testier than ever.

"They're trying to make a national hero out of a guy who hangs over the greatest scorer in hockey," said Reay. "What kind of logic is that? Who pulls them into the stadium — Bobby or this guy Watson? What makes it so great about doing nothing but hanging on a guy all night? So this Watson is a big man."

The biggest man was Roger Crozier, the second-year goaler. He stuffed Hull and the Hawks with a series of acrobatics. The fourth-place Red Wings knocked off the second-place Hawks in six games.

The Red Wings flew off to Montreal for the Finals.

It was amazing. The Red Wings won the first two games in the Forum.

They beat Jean Beliveau, Henri Richard, Yvon Cournoyer. Crozier was brilliant, and the Red Wings were two games from an upset in the Stanley Cup Finals.

Montreal won the third game in Detroit. Then, in Game 4, on a Sunday in Olympia, the Canadiens' Bobby Rousseau crashed into Crozier in the goalie's crease. Crozier suffered a wrenched knee. The Canadiens squared the series against Hank Bassen, who had seldom played all season.

They also won Game 5 back in the Forum.

"Detroit has lost its speed," said Gump Worsley, the Canadiens' goalie, in 1966 press reports. "Howe is the greatest player I ever faced. But Gordie doesn't have the steam he once did. Age has taken its toll."

Howe was 38 at the time. He rallied the Red Wings in Game 6 back in Detroit, with Crozier returned from the wounded. Montreal scored twice — and it seemed the Canadiens had the Cup clinched.

But then Howe fed Delvecchio, who fed Normie Ullman for a goal. They tied the game with under 10 minutes left in the third on Floyd Smith's goal.

Crozier was marvelous. The game went into overtime. Dave Balon slipped the puck to Henri Richard. Richard was toppled over. He reached out his arm and somehow shoved the puck at Crozier.

The red light blinked. The Canadiens had won the Cup. On a fluke goal, probably illegal.

" ... I took Henri Richard down and he put the puck in with his elbow," said Gary Bergman years later. "Or his arm. Or his hand."

Bergman was a young defenseman. "We had our hand on the Cup. We went from the ultimate high to the pits," he said. "That's what made the last goal so devastating."

In defeat, Crozier was awarded the Conn Smythe Trophy as the playoffs' MVP.

The Red Wings would not again reach the Stanley Cup finals for 29 years.

From 1966 to 1995. They would fail to reach the playoffs 15 times in the next 17 years. From 1967 through 1983.

In that long period of inertia, there would be comedy and pathos, weirdness and heroics. There would be years of ineffectual drafts.

In one enormous deal in 1968, the Red Wings traded Normie Ullman, one of their finest shotmakers, to the Maple Leafs. It was a seven-player deal. The Red Wings obtained Frank Mahovlich, a gem of a player who did not sparkle in Detroit. The Wings also got Carl Brewer, young Garry Unger and Peter Stemkowski. They had to give up Paul Henderson and Floyd Smith along with Ullman. The deal backfired on the Red Wings.

After 10 1/2 seasons, Abel gave up the coaching portion of his dual job in 1968-69. Gadsby was the new coach. He remained coach through

the season and, after two games of the following season, owner Bruce Norris fired him.

Abel returned.

"We wanted a more sophisticated coach," Norris explained. It hadn't mattered that the two games Gadsby coached at the start of the 1969-70 season were victories for the Red Wings.

In 1970, Norris hired Ned Harkness as the coach. Harkness had been a college coach at Cornell and Rensselaer Poly. He was now supposed to tell Gordie Howe how to play hockey.

Norris loaded his front office. The office politics stifled the franchise. In the middle of his first season, Harkness succeeded in getting Abel ousted as general manager. Harkness became GM. The period became known as Darkness With Harkness. Howe retired, was taken as a token into the front office, before he left in disgust.

"Check how many vice-presidents there are in the building," he said the night of his Mushroom Treatment speech. The count was seven. They were known as the Silver Shovels — for what they dumped on Howe.

"There's no way I can go back to Olympia and pretend I like those people," Howe said.

They were now cut off from their historic roots. There were some individual exploits in the dark 1970's.

In all his prolific years, Howe had

Brad Park was appointed Red Wings coach when Harry Neale was fired during the 1985-86 season.

never scored 50 goals. Mickey Redmond became the first to hit the half-century in 1972-73 with 52. He scored 51 the following season. Danny Grant scored 50 and Marcel Dionne 47 in 1974-75.

But in none of those seasons could the Red Wings lift them-selves into the playoffs. The game had changed, opened up after expansion. Harkness was dumped. There was a procession of coaches — Doug Barkley, Johnny Wilson, Ted Garvin, Alex Delvecchio, Barkley again, Delvecchio again, Billy Dea, Larry Wilson, Bobby Kromm, Marcel Pronovost.

Garvin made it through 11 games at the start of the 1973-74 season. His record was 2-8-1. His last night, word filtered around Olympia that Garvin would be fired after the game. He must have tuned in on the information. When the game ended, in Detroit defeat, there was no coach behind the bench.

Garvin had vanished, skedaddled before it was over.

The highlight of the 1970's was Kromm's 1977-78 team. It managed to finish second in the Norris Division, merely 51 points behind Scotty Bowman's dynasty-running Canadiens.

Lo and behold, the Red Wings actually beat the Canadiens in the first playoff game in the Forum. Deja vu. The Canadiens won the next four. For his efforts, Kromm was fired during the next season.

The procession continued into the 80's. Lindsay tried it, as coach and GM, and left in frustration. Then Wayne Maxner coached, then Billy Dea one more time.

At last Bruce Norris sold the franchise. The Norris family had operated the Red Wings for 50 years, in great success, then shameful failure.

Mike Ilitch purchased the Red Wings on June 22, 1982. He made Jimmy Devellano the general manager, Nick Polano the coach. The turmoil would continue, even as the Red Wings gradually became respectable again.

At the entry draft of 1983, the Red Wings drafted an 18-year-old center from Ottawa. His name was Steve Yzerman. He was the fourth junior player selected. He was a

bashful, quiet lad.

The Red Wings placed him in the NHL immediately, despite his tender age.

He scored one goal and set up another in his first NHL game against Winnipeg.

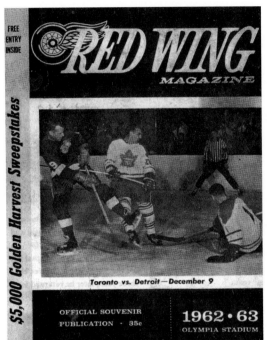

At the season's end, the rookie had 39 goals and 48 assists and the Red Wings were in the playoffs for the first time in six years.

The procession of coaches continued under Iltich and Devellano. Polano gave way to Harry Neale, who was fired after 35 games in 1985-86. Brad Park coached the last 45 — and was fired.

Ilitch hired Jacques Demers in 1986. He had been a successful coach at St. Louis. Ilitch actually pirated him from the Blues. Demers

made Yzerman the Red Wings' captain — at age 21.

In Demers' first season, the Red Wings finished second in the Norris Division. They bumped off the Blackhawks and the Maple Leafs, and reached the Final Four for the Stanley Cup.

They were not ready.

The Edmonton Oilers, with Wayne Gretzky and Mark Messier, beat the Red Wings in the Western Conference Finals. But it was progress.

The next season, 1988-89, the Red Wings finished first in the division.

Yzerman scored 65 goals. They made it back to the Western Finals.

One night in Edmonton, several of the Red Wings broke curfew, visiting an establishment on the edge of town called Goose Loonies. Bob Probert, with his drinking problems, was in the group. Demers had lost his grasp on his team.

Again the Oilers beat them in five games.

The Red Wings became aggressive in their signings. In a cloak-and-dagger scenario, they signed Sergei Fedorov, their first Russian. After the Red Wings fell to fifth place and missed the 1991 playoffs, Ilitch fired Demers.

The procession continued.

Bryan Murray came in as coach/GM. Murray arrived with baggage from a stint in Washington — a fine coach who couldn't win in the playoffs. That first season, Murray's Red Wings finished first again.

But in the playoffs, they struggled through seven games before beating Minnesota, with considerable help from Fedorov. But then the Blackhawks beat them in a sweep. In 1992-93, the Maple Leafs upset the Red Wings in the first round of the playoffs.

Ilitch moved again. He hired Scotty Bowman, who had coached six Stanley Cup championship teams in Montreal and Pittsburgh, as coach. Murray would remain one season in a shaky alliance with Bowman.

In Bowman's first season, 1993-94, the Red Wings again finished first.

They were deemed championship quality. Fedorov scored 56 goals and was the most valuable player in the NHL, the Hart Trophy winner.

In the playoffs he scored one goal. The Red Wings were ousted in the first round by the lowly, expansion San Jose Sharks in seven games. The curse had lasted through 40 seasons.

With Murray gone, and Bowman in power, the Red Wings finished first in the entire NHL in 1995. The battled through the playoffs — and for the first time since Henri Richard's fluke goal in 1966, they reached the Stanley Cup Finals.

There was hysteria in Detroit. Yzerman skated around with the Campbell Cup, the trophy awarded to the Western Conference champi-

ons. The team posed for pictures in the dressing room.

Detroit was favored to win the Cup over the New Jersey Devils. The Devils had once been termed a "Mickey Mouse Team" by Wayne Gretzky. They had no tradition, no championships, no roots.

They swept the Red Wings in four games. The curse continued.

In 1995-96, the Red Wings were primed. With much publicity, with five Russians now unified, the Red Wings won 62 games. It was the most ever by a team, breaking the NHL standard of Bowman's own 1976-77 Canadiens.

The momentum and euphoria carried the Red Wings along in the playoffs to the Western Conference Finals. They had built a hate rivalry with the Colorado Avalanche. The Avalanche upset the Red Wings in six games, with Patrick Roy stopping them — and Claude Lemieux cracking Kris Draper into the boards. The cheap shot was repeated on Detroit TV for weeks, to the pain of every hockey fan. The curse still continued.

First place and regular season records had not worked for the Red Wings.

Bowman planned a gentler pace for 1996-97. Detroit fretted as the Red Wings finished second in the division, third in the West.

In late March, they played the Avalanche at Joe Louis Arena. In a brawl ignited by slender Igor Lari-

onov, the Red Wings took on their archrivals.

Darren McCarty pounded Lemieux into the fetal position. Mike Vernon outpunched Roy bloody in a fight of two goalies. The Red Wings won the game on McCarty's overtime goal.

They were ready for the playoffs.

They beat St.Louis in the first round, with Yzerman's oratory boosting the team when it was down. They swept Anaheim. And then they rallied to eliminate the Avalanche.

They were back in the Finals against the Philadelphia Flyers. Philly was favored.

The Red Wings won the first three games with ease, Yzerman and Joey Kocur scoring nifty goals to establish the mood in Game 1.

And then on Saturday night, June 7, 1997, at Joe Louis Arena the Red Wings completed the sweep of the Flyers, 2-1, with McCarty zigzagging in for the clincher.

Yzerman jumped into Vernon's arms. Then Yzerman was presented with the Stanley Cup. He skated around the ice, through the confetti, in the ritual ride. Larionov and Slava Fetisov skated with it in tandem. Scotty Bowman donned skates and took the Cup for a jaunt. They all skated with it. Vernon was presented with the Conn Smythe Trophy as playoffs MVP.

And 42 years later, as Detroit danced, Ted Lindsay, Gordie Howe and Gary Bergman sat in the stands with their special memories.

Steve Yzerman (left) and the Wings lit up Montreal's Patrick Roy for nine goals on 26 shots.

RED WINGS SAY GOODBYE IN A BIG WAY

Detroit Turns Final Game at Forum into a Laugher

By John Niyo
The Detroit News

The Detroit Red Wings paid their last respects to the fabled Montreal Forum in rather unusual fashion Saturday.

They won a game. And they did it with ease.

Detroit, which hadn't won in Montreal since

RED WINGS
11
—
CANADIENS
1

Montreal,
Dec. 2, 1995

Feb. 6, 1988, skated to an 11-1 victory in what likely will be its only visit this season to the historic old building, which is scheduled to close in mid-March.

By the time the Wings reached double figures, Slava Kozlov had scored four goals for his second career hat trick, Greg Johnson had two goals and an assist,

Sergei Fedorov and Paul Coffey had three assists apiece, and 19-year-old rookie Mathieu Dandenault — a Montreal native with his own cheering section — had one goal as well.

The Wings won their fourth in a row, and 11th in 12 games. Detroit entered Saturday 0-7-1 in its last eight games in Montreal.

Saturday's game was essentially over after the opening period,

as Detroit scored three power-play goals and took a 5-1 lead into the first intermission. A five-minute major assessed to Montreal's Patrick Brisebois (checking from behind) with 49 seconds still remaining on a Wings' power play proved to be the telling blow.

Nicklas Lidstrom scored 11 seconds into the 5-on-3, and the Wings scored twice more on Brisebois' penalty — Johnson with 59 seconds left in the first period, and Kozlov two minutes into the second.

Darren McCarty was injured on Brisebois' check and did not return to the game.

It got so bad that the Forum crowd began to cheer derisively whenever Patrick Roy made a save. He was not the beloved "St. Patrick" on this night, allowing nine goals on 26 shots before being pulled midway through the second.

Mike Vernon, making his second straight start in net, got the victory.

Fedorov's goal at 11:57 of the second period made it 10-1. The only other time Detroit has

Beating Patrick Roy wasn't always as easy as the 11-1 shellacking of Montreal; a victory over Roy's Colorado team put the Wings in the Cup Finals.

scored 10 against the Canadiens was during World War II — Jan. 4, 1942 in Detroit.

Igor Larionov — leading the Wings' Russian charge — got things started, stuffing home a rebound off his own miss. The goal came with a man-advantage after Valeri Bure was sent off for hooking.

Larionov set up the next goal, as well. Vladimir Konstantinov picked up a loose puck in Montreal's zone and fed Larionov, who threaded a pass to Kozlov waiting alone at the far post. The goal, at 8:21, was easy.

Mark Recchi scored less than a minute later on a Canadiens' power play to make it 2-1.

But Kozlov answered at 10:13 with his second goal of the night. He shot from just inside the blue line, sending the puck past a screened Roy.

The Forum crowd — including a sizable Detroit contingent — was on its feet early.

Less than 30 seconds after the opening faceoff, McCarty and Montreal's Turner Stevenson dropped the gloves and squared off.

That came moments after a more civil affair. The Canadiens held a pre-game ceremony to honor Detroit's final visit to the Forum, a ceremony they will repeat for all of the original six NHL teams.

COFFEY REACHES 1,000 BEFORE JOE LOUIS CROWD

Defenseman's Assist Milestone Overshadows Probert's Return

By Cynthia Lambert
The Detroit News

It had been anticipated. Finally, it happened.

No, the reference is not to Bob Probert's less-than-enthusiastic return to Joe Louis Arena in the Red Wings' 3-1 victory over the Blackhawks Wednesday night.

It's to gifted defenseman Paul Coffey finally getting his 1,000th assist, and he did it where he wanted to do — in front of the home crowd.

"It was perfect," Coffey said. "It's been a while: I really wanted to get it in New York (last Friday, when he also got No. 999). But this was perfect."

He didn't make the fans wait, either. With 30.8 seconds left in the first period, and Chicago leading 1-0, Coffey set up Igor Larionov for the tying goal. But more poignantly, the assist made Coffey the first defenseman ever to reach 1,000 assists. Only three other players have made it to quadruple digits — Gordie Howe, Wayne Gretzky and

BLACKHAWKS

1

RED WINGS

3

Detroit,
Dec. 13, 1995

Marcel Dionne.

"He's probably been the best offensive defenseman ever to play this game," Chicago coach Craig Hartburg said. "Well, he is. Bobby Orr's career was cut short."

As for Probert, no, he didn't fight. Didn't even come close. The 19,983 in attendance also did not give him a hero's welcome, much to their credit. In fact, more fans booed the former Red Wings enforcer than cheered him.

Probert, through a team spokesman, declined to talk with reporters after the game, which seemed appropriate. This night belonged to the current Red Wings, who lead the Western Conference thanks to a 15-2 run in the last month or so.

"I don't want to be overconfident," Larionov said. "Because this is the NHL and you have to play 100 percent all the time. Of course, it's hard to stop us when we are playing so well. We are playing so well together."

Coffey, who knows a thing or two

about winning — and winning it all, concurred with Larionov.

"We're playing really well as a team," Coffey said. "I've said it before and I'm not going to say it again ... we had a bad week and a half (in the finals last spring). It reminded me of the 1986 playoffs when Calgary beat us (Edmonton) in seven games. It's very similar. But now we're getting that team effort from everyone. In the first period tonight, Ozzie held us in there. That's his job."

Goalie Chris Osgood indeed kept the Wings in the game for the bulk of the first period, when the Blackhawks were their most dangerous.

Even during a five-minute Detroit power play, Chicago threatened more, managing two shots on net to Detroit's three. Osgood's best save occurred at 16:40 of the first, when he stopped ex-Red Wing Joe Murphy on a breakaway, coming out of the net to cut the angle.

"It was good in the first period," Osgood said. "I got some shots. I'm supposed to play well. That's my job."

"But they were pretty fired up in

the first and we knew that they would be. But in the second and third, we were outstanding."

In addition to Larionov, Tim Taylor and Keith Primeau scored for the Wings. Murphy got the Blackhawks' goal.

Instead of a joyous homecoming for Probert, Wednesday's game had more of a reminiscent tone from last spring's playoffs. Intensity and focus were the bywords as the teams met for the first time since the Wings won the Western Conference championship in five games.

Probert made his first appearance 33 seconds into the first period.

He stepped onto the ice to a lukewarm reception by some, and was booed by many others.

Any cheers there might have been were easily drowned out by the louder fans who weren't prepared to openly welcome the former Detroit bad boy back to town.

When Probert got his first shot on net, three minutes into the first, there was an enthusiastic cheer for Osgood making the save.

Murphy scored at 19:03 of the first, and Larionov's goal tied it at 19:29.

As the players poured onto the ice to congratulate Coffey, Hartsburg lobbied for a delay-of-game call — to no avail.

The off-ice officials said the Wings received special permission to come onto the ice when Coffey got the 1,000th.

Coffey Finds 1,000-Assist Hubbub 'Overwhelming'

By John Niyo
The Detroit News

It was nothing he hadn't done a thousand or so times before. Nine hundred ninety-nine to be exact. And thousands more in practice and as a youngster.

Carry the puck up the middle, across the blue line, veer to the left to let the others catch up, pause, then deliver the pass. Right on the tape.

But Paul Coffey will remember this one. He got the 1,000th assist of his career Wednesday night against Chicago. Milestones like this you cherish forever.

"It's kind of overwhelming," said Coffey, admitting that it hasn't sunk in yet even though he was mobbed by TV cameras and reporters in the locker room after the game. "I suppose it's something I'll reflect on when it's all over."

One thousand assists. It's a feat accomplished by three others in the history of the National Hockey League: Wayne Gretzky (1,725 and counting), Gordie Howe (1,049) and Marcel Dionne (1,040). None of those three is a defenseman, which is why Coffey with that nonchalant flick of the wrist Wednesday night assured himself of a special place in hockey lore.

Gretzky, one of his closest friends, let him know exactly that as soon as he could.

"After the first period, Paul (Boyer, the equipment manager) came over and said, 'There's a phone call for you.' It was Wayne. He was watching in L.A. in the dressing room.

"He said, 'I wanted to be the first to congratulate you ... You've only got 500 or 600 more to go to catch me.'"

Coffey laughed and sighed, the weight of a thousand assists lifted from his shoulders.

"I wanted to do it here at home," said Coffey, whose five-game point streak (which included nine assists) ended Tuesday in St. Louis. "I couldn't have planned it any better."

But the ovation left him a little bewildered.

"I'm not very good at (that) stuff," he said.

WINGS ALIVE AFTER 2-OT THRILLER

Yzerman's Goal Puts Away Blues in Game 7, Sends Detroit to Conference Finals

By Cynthia Lambert
The Detroit News

The irony was inescapable.

"He kept saying he didn't care who scored and he's the one who did," said Wings coach Scotty Bowman of Steve Yzerman's goal 1:15 into the second overtime Thursday night.

The goal gave the Red Wings a 1-0 victory over the St. Louis Blues in Game 7 of the Western Conference semifinals.

It was the Red Wings' first victory in a Game 7 in three recent tries. They lost in 1994 to San Jose and in 1993 to Toronto. Granted, it took double-overtime, but the Wings will take it.

The goal, scored on Yzerman's eighth shot of the night, not only

BLUES

0

RED WINGS

1

Detroit,
May 16, 1996

gave the Red Wings the victory, but enabled them to advance to the Western Conference finals against the Colorado Avalanche.

The series begins at 3 p.m. Sunday at Joe Louis Arena.

"Yeah, that's the most exciting goal I've scored," said Yzerman, the Wings' top playoff scorer with eight goals and 17 points.

The shutout was goaltender Chris Osgood's second of the playoffs.

"It feels good, that's all," Osgood said, "I think a win like this shows that this team has grown. There was no negative thinking going on."

Vladimir Konstantinov sent Yzerman in when he made a long pass to the Detroit captain through the neutral zone.

Wayne Gretzky nearly intercepted the pass, but once the puck got to Yzerman, he was off and skating. When he passed the blue line on the right side, he let loose a shot that beat goalie Jon Casey high.

"I didn't have great speed, but I had some," Yzerman said. "I felt I could get it away. I wasn't thinking score, I was thinking of getting it by the defenseman.

"I know the play was to get it in deep, but I did have some speed and I wanted to get a shot away."

And away it went. The scene was a flash compared to the prime scoring chances the Red Wings had during the game.

One of their best opportunities came just 14 seconds into the second overtime when Yzerman skated behind the net and shuffled the puck to Sergei Fedorov in the slot. But Casey made the save.

The Wings outshot the Blues, 40-29.

Steve Yzerman celebrates after his slapshot –"the most exciting goal I've scored"– beat Jon Casey in double overtime.

Mike Vernon and Aaron Ward rejoice in the downfall of the arch-rival Avalanche, who eliminated the Wings in 1996.

RED WINGS FLY INTO FINALS AGAINST PHILADELPHIA

Detroit Ousts Colorado in Game 6

By Cynthia Lambert

The Detroit News

Goodbye, Colorado Avalanche. Hello, Philadelphia Flyers.

The Red Wings bade farewell to the Avalanche on Monday night with a 3-1 victory at Joe Louis Arena to advance to the Stanley Cup Finals for the second time in three years.

AVALANCHE
1

RED WINGS
3

Detroit,
May 26, 1997

The Wings clinched the Western Conference finals in six games, the same number Colorado needed last season to eliminate the Wings before winning the Cup. The Wings will open the Finals in Philadelphia on Saturday night.

"We talked about it (Sunday)," Wings Coach Scotty Bowman said. "If you're going to beat a champion, you can't outpoint them. You have to knock them out. We didn't want to go back to Colorado.

"When you can knock out a Stan-

Avalanche goalie Patrick Roy congratulates Steve Yzerman after Detroit's Game 6 victory.

Not a safety net: Steve Yzerman barrels into Avalanche goaltender Patrick Roy.

ley Cup winner with one game, you should do it. You don't want to, when you're my age, be looking back and say you didn't show up for the game. You'd never forgive yourself."

Sergei Fedorov must have been listening to Bowman. He showed up, and risked his body to stay in the game.

At 5:31 of the first period, Fedorov collided with defenseman Aaron Miller, causing Fedorov's elbow to jam into his side. His diaphragm went into spasms, he couldn't catch his breath and he had to leave the game.

Doctors told Bowman after the first period that Fedorov might be able to return for the third. But after being told by captain Steve Yzerman how important he was to the team, Fedorov returned midway through the second with the energy of a player taking his first shift in the season opener.

"I was excited to get back," Fedorov said. "When I got back to the bench, I let everyone know I was there. I started saying, 'Let's do it, let's do it.'"

At 6:11 of the third period, with the Wings leading 1-0, Fedorov did it. He took a pass from Vyacheslav Kozlov and sent a hard shot at Patrick Roy from close range. Roy made the save, but Fedorov scored on the rebound to make it 2-0.

"Sergei is an unbelievable talent," Kris Draper said. "When a player like him gets hurt, you want him back as soon as possible. When he came back, he sat next to me and asked how I felt. I told him I felt great. He said, 'Me too.' When one of your best players says that, that's all you want to hear. Then he comes out and gets the game-winning goal. It was a perfect script for him."

The Wings needed Fedorov's goal because Scott Young scored on a rebound of Adam Deadmarsh's shot at 14:48 of the third to make it 2-1. But the Wings persevered, as they had throughout the series.

Brendan Shanahan scored into an empty net with 29.8 seconds left to make it 3-1 and send the Wings to the Finals for the 20th time.

"It was such a relief to get that empty-netter," Shanahan said. "Now it's back to work. The Stanley Cup still hasn't been won."

But the Wings will take something more to the Finals than memories of holding the Clarence Campbell bowl. They will take an improved, and wiser, team.

"I think we played better than them," Martin Lapointe said of the Avalanche. "It's nice to see they couldn't step up. We beat them on the boards, to the puck. We showed a lot of heart tonight."

The same could not be said of the Avalanche, who were outshot, 42-

16. Roy was outstanding in keeping his team in the game.

"Patrick kept us in it and gave us a chance to steal one," Avalanche coach Marc Crawford said. "But at this point in the year, you don't steal one. The whole group of us has to take a big, long look in the mirror and learn the lessons."

Said the Wings' Darren McCarty: "We had so many opportunities throughout the game to win it. Hats off to Patrick Roy. He played outstanding."

The Wings recovered from a 6-0 loss in Game 5 Saturday night in Denver. Not only did they want to end the series at home, they also desperately wanted to avoid returning to Denver, where the Avalanche were 8-1 in the postseason.

"I think that's a safe assumption," McCarty said. "When you have the opportunity to win a series at home, you've got to do it.

"This is really such a great feeling. But Joey (Kocur) said it all when we were huddled around after the game. He said, 'Don't worry, boys, the next one feels even better.'"

The next one would be the Stanley Cup, which has eluded the Red Wings since 1955 — the longest drought in the NHL.

A 42-16 Wings' shots advantage was simply too much for goalie Patrick Roy and the Avalanche to overcome.

Bowman Hard-headed and Successful in Coaching Seven Stanley Cup Champions

By Jerry Green
The Detroit News

I
t is a dangerous game. The players carry clubs in their hands. They wear honed steel blades as sharp as knives on their feet. They dash crazily on ice and shoot a galvanized rubber disc wildly at speeds above 100 miles an hour. In an earlier era, they did not wear protective helmets.

It is the game Scotty Bowman aspired to play in the National Hockey League, since he was a wee lad in an English-speaking neighborhood of Montreal. He possessed the talent for the game. It was evident he was NHL material by the time he reached junior hockey in his late teens.

Then — Bowman relishes retelling his life story — the accident that turned him into coaching. He sat one day during hockey season in the back room where the Red Wings coaches view videos and diagram defenses. The room is reporter-proof. A rare invitation was issued. And he spoke:

"I got my first skates when I was maybe seven. That was pretty young in those days. You didn't get on teams until you were around 12. I got on

a team when I was around 10. I played when I was seven, but we didn't have organized teams.

"I got on a group team when I was about 14. We won the whole province of Quebec midget championship."

He advanced to the Montreal Royals, the Canadiens' top junior club. One day, on the ice, there was a collision. Two players carrying those clubs, riding on those steel knife-sharp blades. Bowman received a severe whack in the head. His skull was shattered. His career ambitions were crushed.

He loved hockey so he steered into coaching, where he would become an immortal. He would coach the great Canadiens to five Stanley Cup champions in his native Montreal. He would coach the Pittsburgh Penguins to another Stanley Cup championship in 1992. And at age 63, after bitter disappointments, he would recreate, mastermind, tinker with the Red Wings until they were molded into his ideal of a championship team. And they would win the Stanley Cup in 1997 for the first time in 42 years.

Coach of seven Stanley Cup champions, player development director of another, the ironic result of a knock in the head. Only Toe Blake, of the

Scotty Bowman can have mysterious sides, even to those who know him best.

mighty Canadiens in the 1950's and 60's, coached more Stanley Cup champions than Bowman, eight.

"A player was all I wanted to be," he said, continuing his story in the back room in the bowels of Joe Louis Arena. "I went to high school but ... Actually when I got injured, I was still in high school. It was my senior year. I was playing junior hockey. I got injured March 7, 1951. I was 18½."

There was a skirmish. Scotty was hit over the head by a stick. He fell to the ice, badly hurt. The player who whacked Bowman over the head with the hockey stick was a young defenseman, Jean-Guy Talbot. Bowman would never forget the name.

Young coaches are required to begin at the bottom, the roots of hockey across Canada. Bowman started with kids' hockey, junior B's, juniors in Ottawa, the Peterborough Petes, the junior Canadiens. In 1967, the NHL expanded, doubled in size from The Original Six. There were six head coaching positions instantly available.

Bowman was hired by Lynn Patrick to coach the new St. Louis Blues.

His players were craggy veterans, their careers prolonged by new job opportunities. Bowman had two brilliant hockey Hall of Famers to play goal, Glenn Hall and Jacques Plante. He had Dickie Moore and Doug Harvey, two aging players from the Canadiens past champions.

But in this first season, Bowman sought another veteran defenseman.

Bowman went with Mike Vernon — and not Chris Osgood — in the playoffs, a move that helped the Wings win the Stanley Cup.

Steve Yzerman changed his style of play under Bowman, and it brought him his cherished Stanley Cup.

He scanned the NHL's waiver wire. He picked a name.

The player he brought to the blues was an ornery craggy, tough, veteran defenseman. His name was Jean-Guy Talbot.

The irony was rich. They never discussed the incident that had terminated Bowman's career as a player at its beginning 16 years earlier.

He developed the elderly Blues into a team that reached the Stanley Cup Finals in the first three years of their existence. The NHL, in its desire to market the United States,

rigged the playoffs so that an American expansion club would reach the Finals every year. Scotty's Blues never won a game against the established Canadiens or Bruins in three championship series.

But he was established as an NHL coach. His jut-jawed image, head held upward, reaching down for an ice cube to munch, would become a television caricature for more than a quarter century.

Bowman was coveted by Charles O. Finley to coach the California Seals and Jack Kent Cooke to coach

the Los Angeles Kings. He rejected both owners. He would ultimately return to Montreal. He had proven, in signing Talbot, that he did not necessarily have to love his players to win. Many of them have proven through the years that they certainly didn't love him.

In Detroit, there was a huge generation gap. Bowman had the credentials, he had the hockey knowledge, but it was uncertain that he had the knack to handle athletes 35 and 40 years younger than he was. He has been successful through the

1960's, an era of young rage, and the 1970's, 80's into the 90's. The character of North American youth changed. Salaries climbed and climbed. Athletes needed pampering. The dressing room often turned into a sandbox.

Plus there was another gap. This gap was transoceanic. The Red Wings were avidly signing Europeans. They brought in players from Sweden. When the Soviet Union crumbled in 1989, skillful Russian hockey players suddenly found they were free to become millionaires. The Red Wings quickly signed players from Moscow's famed CSKA champions, the noted Red Army team. They picked off Sergei Fedorov, Vladimir Konstantinov, Vyacheslav Kozlov. All for free. Valerie Gushin, the general manager of the Red Army team in Moscow, cried American piracy. The Red Wings laughed in response.

Bowman handled athletes of mixed personalities, sulkers and carousers, for 25 years in the NHL. But Russians — and the Red Wings would have a Russian Five when they won the Stanley Cup — would be a different sort of challenge.

Sitting in the room, Bowman pointed to one of the five Russians.

Bowman got the last laugh against Colorado coach Marc Crawford in the Western Conference Finals.

"He had a lifestyle orgasm," Bowman said. "He had no idea five years ago he'd have what he has now."

When Bowman arrived in Detroit in 1993, he had just won his sixth Cup as a coach in Pittsburgh. He became the Detroit coach with the simple mandate from franchise owner Mike Ilitich:

"Win the Cup."

It took four seasons of grooming, retooling, cajoling, surviving front office politics — and changing some playing lifestyles. It took four years of carping, and rumors, from much of the media. It took four years of playing goalkeeper tag.

"My idol in hockey was Toe Blake," said Bowman. "But the coach I admired was Don Shula. He lasted a long time. He had to change styles."

But more often, Bowman had been compared to another historic, despotic football coach in moods, temperament, handling of athletes.

"He is the best coach in any sport since Vince Lombardi," a journalist familiar with both eras said during the 1996-97 season.

It was the ultimate compliment.

Bowman's first three seasons with the Red Wings were shocking, disappointing, frustrating, controversial, at times angry.

Ilitch hired Bowman after Jacques Demers and then Bryan Murray were given the ziggy — a Detroit-only word that translates to an unceremonious firing. Demers and

Murray had moderate success. Murray spent three years as coach and general manager. After failures in the playoffs, he was replaced by Bowman, but retained the GM's position.

The Red Wings had stars. Bowman inherited Steve Yzerman, the club's captain. At the time, Yzerman was regarded in the same scoring echelon as Mario Lemieux and Wayne Gretzky. Yzerman had seasons in which he had scored 50, 65, 62, 51 and 58 goals.

One of Bowman's first acts was to change Yzerman's style. A swift, elusive skater, Bowman had Yzerman concentrate on defense.

The Red Wings finished first in the Western Conference in Bowman's first season. They were humiliated in the first round of the playoffs by the lightweight San Jose Sharks.

Ilitch impatiently courted Mike Keenan, who had just won the Cup with the Rangers, to switch to Detroit as coach. The Blues outbid the Red Wings for Keenan. Bowman survived.

What the Red Wings had was two coach/GM types, Bowman and Murray. One naturally had to go. Murray was fired. Bowman assumed his basic duties as director of player personnel.

His second season, the Red Wings reached the Cup Finals for the first time in 29 years. Detroit was agog with hockey enthusiasm. The Red Wings were favored to win the

Stanley Cup against the New Jersey Devils, once referred to as "a Mickey Mouse team" by Wayne Gretzky. Detroit hadn't won it since 1955. The Devils blew the Red Wings out in a horrendous four-game sweep.

Shawn Burr was made the scapegoat. He was traded to Tampa Bay.

Burr told The St. Petersburg Times what happened once when Bowman called him for an opinion of the coaching.

"Scotty, you're 60 years old," Burr was quoted as saying. "You play with toy trains. You use a duck call to make line changes. People call you a genius. I think there's something wrong with you. I think you're a joke."

In Bowman's third season the Red Wings roared through the schedule. They had a target — the magic sports number of 60. In all of NHL history only one club had won 60 games in a season. It was the 1976-77 Canadiens, coached by Scotty Bowman. It was the second of Bowman's four-season Cup dynasty in Montreal. The Red Wings broke the record with 62 victories.

He can be a secretive man with a deep curiosity.

This time the Red Wings were eliminated in a heated, nasty six-game semifinal, or Western Conference final, series with the Colorado Avalanche. Bowman enraged, engaged in a nasty parking lot shouting match in Denver with the Avalanche's Claude Lemieux.

"Nice sucker punch, Lemieux," Bowman was heard to yell from the Red Wings' bus.

For the first time, Marc Crawford, the young Colorado coach, spouted angry remarks at Bowman.

"He's the master of creating a little bit of circus away from the game ... " Crawford told the media.

"He's been doing this thing for years and years and years ...

"He's a great thinker, but he thinks so much that you even get the plate in his head causing interference on our headsets during the game."

It was a cruel remark. One of the myths in the NHL is that Bowman has a plate in his head because of the incident with Talbot.

Some of Bowman's old Montreal players who went on to high posts in hockey spoke with praise. Former All-Star defenseman Larry Robinson is now coach of the Kings.

"Hate is the wrong word, but when he was coaching us, he wasn't a guy you as a player respected," Robinson told The Los Angeles Times. "But you respect him now more that you're through. To you, it's a game. To him, it's much more than that. He's always trying to stay a step ahead. He's constantly thinking of ways to make you a better player. I guess I misunderstood when I was a player. But being in his shoes now, I understand a lot better why he did the things he did."

It was the highest tribute a former player could give to his former coach.

Ken Dryden, Bowman's Montreal goalkeeper, now is boss of the Maple Leafs.

"The only common piece is Scotty Bowman, and that says a lot," Dryden said while the Red Wings were aiming to break the 60-victories record.

Beaten again in the playoffs by Colorado, Bowman again reformed his club for 1996-97. This time the club was created to win the playoffs. The regular season was simply regarded as a testing period. They finished second in the division, third in the conference.

Bowman had a grander scheme. He dealt popular Dino Ciccarelli to Tampa Bay. "He's a jerk," Ciccarelli said publicly. He cashiered Bob Errey. "A man that doesn't respect people should not be given any respect," Errey told The St.Petersburg Times. "Why would you want time for a man like that."

Bowman shrugged off the criticism.

He dealt Paul Coffey and Keith Primeau to Hartford to obtain a huge property the Red Wings desperately needed — Brendan Shanahan. He brought Joey Kocur back from a suburban Detroit beer league to provide muscle. He played the five Russians as a unit — Fedorov, Kozlov, Igor Larionov, Konstantinov, Slava Fetisov. Then he broke them up. Unlike the year before, when he played guessing games whether Chris

Bowman shares a laugh with a former member of the coaching fraternity, television analyst Don Cherry.

Osgood or Mike Vernon would start playoff games, he settled on a single goalkeeper. He relegated the younger Osgood to the bench and went with the experienced Vernon. To shore up the defense, he obtained Larry Murphy from the Maple Leafs.

And when playoffs came, the Red Wings were prepared. They rolled through. They beat St. Louis in six. They swept Anaheim, with three games going into overtime. After a triple overtime victory, Bowman even showed some emotion. He smiled. They evened matters with Colorado, Bowman admonishing Crawford during one evening of belligerence in Joe Louis Arena.

William Scott Bowman, himself, had revered his father. He was the son of a Scottish immigrant in a bilingual city. It is rather difficult to picture Scotty Bowman, as a little boy, playing with the kids down the street, wearing his Boston Bruins' replica jersey, in the 1930's and early 1940's.

Young Scotty Bowman, perverse even as a lad, favored neither the Canadiens nor the Maroons, soon to be disbanded.

"I grew up a Boston Bruin fan," Bowman said in his back room, "the reason being the Boston radio broadcast. You could pick up the signal in Montreal. I think the reason was, I was about seven years old, and they were winning the Cup. The Rangers won it in 1940. Boston won it in '41.

"I used to have to go to bed at the end of the first or second period. My father would always write the score before he went to work the next day.

"I think probably the reason that I was a Boston fan, they were a strong team. One Christmas I got ... somehow they found a Boston Bruins jersey.

"The two jerseys you could buy in Montreal were Canadiens and Toronto. They found a Boston Bruins jersey and they put No. 10 on it for Bill Cowley. That was my big hero. He was a big centerman, as you know. He made more wings than Boeing. From Ottawa. Died a couple of years ago. I visited him.

"There was nobody else around me who followed the Bruins. You're kids, you can't get into much trouble. I used to wear my Boston sweater."

This was Scotty Bowman in his off-ice finest, the raconteur, the historian.

Bowman's street in suburban Verdun was part French-speaking and part-English speaking. He learned both languages, attended a French-speaking school for while. All the kids rooted for the Canadiens and Maroons, except Bowman — and the two kids down the street with their other interests.

"The first game I would have gone to was Canadiens against Maroons," Bowman said, "Because my father was a Maroons fan.

"See, when you grew up in Montreal at that time, most of the English were Maroons fans. The French were for the Canadiens ...

"They had what they called in

Before joining the Red Wings, Bowman won Stanley Cups as a coach with the Montreal Canadiens and the Pittsburgh Penguins.

Montreal at the time, they had a rush end. Fifty cents. They called it Millionaires' Row, but it (cost only) 50 cents.

"I remember my dad waited, he used to line up behind the Forum. Obviously in the middle of winter, and he waited for tickets ... Tickets were sold at the corner of Burnside and Atwater. Right on the corner, they had a little wicket there.

Jack Bowman was a soccer player and a blacksmith by trade in Scot-

land. He emigrated to Canada in 1929. He became a railroad man. In 1930, Bowman's mother, Jean, went to Montreal to marry Jack.

It was from his mother, Jean, that Bowman inherited much of his personality. There were times, it has been reported, that she would respond to weak hands in card games by throwing her cards into the fireplace.

"I grew up on a street, two of the boys became safecrackers," he said once. "They would crack safes. In banks.

"That wasn't the real type of neighborhood it was."

Scotty Bowman did not achieve his boyhood ambition. But his playmates from down the street in Verdun did.

"One ended up in prison in Vancouver," Bowman said, "and the other ended up in the big job (big house) in Boston. They became bank robbers. Armed robbery."

And Bowman collected eight precious Stanley Cup rings.

Bowman joins the Wings in a center-ice celebration following the Finals' sweep of the Philadelphia Flyers.

RED WINGS SOLVE HEX, FLYERS' HEXTALL

Detroit Takes Its First Victory in Finals Since 1966

By Cynthia Lambert

The Detroit News

The Red Wings chased one more ghost from their past on Saturday night, when they defeated the Philadelphia Flyers, 4-2, in Game 1 of the Stanley Cup Finals.

The Detroit franchise won for the first in the Finals since it defeated the Montreal Canadiens on April 26, 1966. That victory gave the Wings a 2-0 series lead, but they ended up losing in six games.

RED WINGS

4

FLYERS

2

Philadelphia,
May 31, 1997

"It's great to win one game," associate coach Dave Lewis said. "Nobody talked about it much, but ... this means a lot to the guys."

The last time the Wings made it this far, they were chased away in four straight by the New Jersey Devils. Since then, the Wings have been waiting to avenge the disgrace. Saturday's victory gave them a start.

"I think it's a huge pat on the back for us," said Mike Vernon, who turned aside 26 shots. "In our series vs. New Jersey, we were very disap-

Ron Hextall was shaky in the Flyers' net, giving up two first-period goals.

Slava Fetisov and the Wings tied up the Flyers for most of Game 1.

pointed and embarrassed by what happened. I can look back now and see that we were beat in every area of the game, not just in goals, but in shots and everything. But we learned a valuable lesson from the Devils, and we bring that into this series."

Of course, after a poor showing in Game 1, the Flyers also have motivation from a negative experience.

"We didn't skate well, we didn't support the puck well," captain Eric Lindros said. "We knew what they were going to do, and we didn't do

what we had to do to counter that."

Instead, the Flyers tried to rely heavily on their size, a plan for which the Wings prepared.

"They're a physical hockey club," Kris Draper said. "I don't know if we outsmarted them as much as out-skated them. I know that's something that I have to do, since most of their guys have 40 or 50 pounds on me. That's my asset."

But scouting also was a Wings asset. Entering the series, they knew the Flyers were vulnerable to defen-

sive lapses. The Wings took advantage of many of those, and exposed Ron Hextall as a goalie they could easily beat — at least on this night.

Hextall gave up first-period goals to Kirk Maltby — the culmination of a two-on-none with Kris Draper — and Joe Kocur, and a second-period goal on a long wrist shot by Sergei Fedorov. But his biggest mistake came on Steve Yzerman's slap shot from the blue line 56 seconds into the third.

The timing of Yzerman's goal was crucial, since it came so quickly into

the final period, when the Flyers had to come out strong.

Vernon preserved the Wings' lead late in the third when he made his best save of the game, on Trent Klatt at 14:22. Klatt, at the right circle, took a pass from Lindros and fired a shot at Vernon. He came out of the net to cut the angle.

"What made that save easier is that Vladimir (Konstantinov) and Stevie (Yzerman) came back to take the pass back away," Vernon said. "I thought Klatt might try to go back to Lindros, but they covered that. I came out and got my glove on the puck."

Rod Brind'Amour (power play) and John LeClair scored for the Flyers. Brind'Amour's came in the first period, and at first it appeared as if Yzerman had scored inadvertently. But Yzerman said Brind'Amour had extended his stick to tap the puck past Vernon during a flurry in front of the net.

LeClair scored late in the second to trim the Wings' lead to 3-2 entering the third. But Yzerman's goal distanced the Flyers again.

The Flyers were never able to try to pull Hextall from the net for the extra attacker. Lindros took a frustration penalty at 17:48 when he slugged Konstantinov in the face, basically sending the Wings on the power play for the rest of the game.

Brendan Shanahan (14), brought to the Wings in the Paul Coffey trade, leaves Coffey smarting.

RED WINGS' CUP HALF FULL; FLYERS BOW AT HOME AGAIN

Odds Favor Detroit with 2-0 Series Lead

Mike Vernon (14-4 in the playoffs) continues to play tough in the nets. "I'm just trying to get myself in good position," he said.

By Cynthia Lambert
The Detroit News

The Red Wings played their way into superb position Tuesday night, defeating the Philadelphia Flyers, 4-2, at the CoreStates Center to take a two-games-to-none lead in the best-of-seven Stanley Cup Finals.

RED WINGS
4
——
FLYERS
2
Philadelphia,
June 3, 1997

The Wings return to Joe Louis Arena for games 3 and 4 on Thursday and Saturday with the odds of winning the series in their favor. Only three times since 1939 have teams rallied from a 2-0 deficit to win a Finals series, and only twice has a team lost the first two at home and won the series.

"We know the position we're in," defenseman Bob Rouse said. "We realize now we're that much closer and that we've put ourselves in a good position. But there's a lot of fight left in the Flyers and we know that, too."

Tomas Sandstrom is on the receiving end of rare Philadephia rough stuff in the Finals.

The Wings also know what the Flyers are up against. In 1995, the Wings lost the first two games at home to the New Jersey Devils in the Finals, and were swept.

"The hunger level for us elevates now," said Brendan Shanahan, who scored twice. "We know winning on the road doesn't mean anything unless you can do it at home, too. There's a lot of hockey left in front of us yet."

Not if Philadelphia can't find better goaltending.

As in Game 1, soft goals allowed by the Flyers helped the Wings win. In Game 2, Garth Snow — not Ron Hextall — was the culprit.

"We have to have a higher responsibility to ... play better and it starts with the goaltender," Flyers coach Terry Murray said. "We had too many breakdowns and too many turnovers. That, and not getting big stops, are the biggest nightmare for a team in the Stanley Cup Finals."

Goaltending also was the story for the Wings. Mike Vernon was outstanding, making big saves throughout.

"I don't know what the perception is out there," Wings defenseman Larry Murphy said. "But anybody in this room definitely hasn't overlooked Mike and what he's done for us. The guys in here are thankful for him being there. In the room after the first two games, everyone's

come in and gone over and patted Mike on the back because we know what he's done for us."

Coach Scotty Bowman said Vernon was a key against the Flyers.

"He's an experienced goalie and the Flyers get a lot of people in front because of their size," Bowman said. "So for him it's a case of knowing when to cover the bottom of the net or when to freeze the puck. He's handling the puck very well in this series, and that has helped our defensemen because I thought tonight their shoot-ins were better than they were in the first game."

Vernon, who is 14-4 in the playoffs this year, said he is playing the game he has always played.

Replacing ineffective Ron Hextall in the net, the Flyers' Garth Snow had no better success in Game 2.

"I'm just trying to get myself in good position," he said. "I'm not the type of goaltender to come way out of the net. I'm just trying to hold my ground."

Steve Yzerman had a power-play goal and Kirk Maltby also scored for the Wings. Shanahan's first goal and Maltby's were on shots from beyond the top of the faceoff circles.

Detroit led, 3-2, after two periods, and made it 4-2 thanks to a breakdown in the Philadelphia defense. The Wings got a two-on-one break, with Paul Coffey as the only Flyer back. Martin Lapointe, closing on the right, passed to Shanahan, whose shot from the left

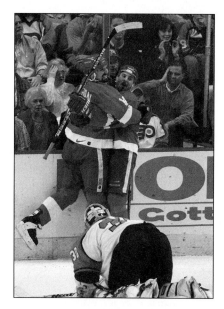

Brendan Shanahan celebrates one of his two goals in Game 2.

dot beat Snow.

Rod Brind'Amour scored two power-play goals on high deflections. But the goals weren't enough to offset a poor performance by Snow, who started after Hextall's subpar performance in Game 1.

"It seems like we're always chasing from behind," Flyers forward Mikael Renberg said. "That's a tough way to play."

Had the Flyers received better goaltending from Snow, the outcome might have been different. Unlike Game 1, the Flyers used their speed and were successful at dumping the puck in the Wings' zone and keeping it there with strong forechecking.

Both Wings new — Larry Murphy — and old — Steve Yzerman — contributed with strong Game 2 efforts, with Yzerman scoring a power-play goal.

The Flyers' speed was boosted by lineup changes, and they tied the score despite the Wings taking a 2-0 lead by 9:22 of the first period.

"They did a few adjustments in the first half of the game," Bowman said. "I thought they made shorter passes. They had more speed through the neutral zone and we got trapped a few times. But I think we adjusted. We did adjust in the third period pretty well."

One of the Wings' best adjustments was something they have worked on throughout the playoffs. Even when the Flyers pressed, the Wings withstood the pressure because of tight checking and strong goaltending.

"I think we were able to remain composed throughout the game," Yzerman said. "Our goaltender made some real good saves. Our defensemen, I thought, were real solid in front of the net in blocking some shots and clearing pucks out. I don't think that we controlled the game by any means, but we were able to remain relatively composed when the heat got on us."

The Wings return to Detroit with a chance to take a commanding series lead Thursday night. Although his team is in dire straits, Flyers captain Eric Lindros placed the pressure on the Wings.

"We haven't had a lead to work with yet," Lindros said. "But the pressure is on them with a 2-0 lead. They are supposed to win it. We'll go to Detroit and see what happens."

RED WINGS HAMMER FLYERS, FEEL A SWEEPING SENSATION

Stanley Cup Seems an Inevitable Victory Away

By Bob Wojnowski

The Detroit News

This isn't about Philadelphia now, not that it ever was. The Flyers are still out there simply because the NHL requires an opponent, to make it official.

The Red Wings are skating alone now, chasing something only they and their fans can truly see and understand. This is how a 42-year wait ends, with a pursuit so dogged, so dominating, it hardly matters who's on the other side.

Three periods of formality Saturday night are all that stand between the Wings and a sweep to the Stanley Cup, a distance reduced to the slimmest margin because the Wings will not let up, not for one second or one shift. They belted the Flyers, 6-1, Thursday night to seize a 3-0 lead in the Finals, and they did it as they've done it all playoffs, with a disciplined defense, with help from every area, led by the captain, who has scored in all three games.

FLYERS

1

RED WINGS

6

Detroit,
June 5, 1997

Steve Yzerman bagged the first goal, Sergei Fedorov and Martin Lapointe had two apiece and by the end, the fans were feasting, famished by the wait. As the lead mounted, they cheered huge hits by Vladimir Konstantinov, an assist by Mike Vernon on the sixth goal and a circus shot by Brendan Shanahan, who scored from behind the net, flipping the puck off beleaguered goalie Ron Hextall.

Obviously, the Flyers have no one to stop the puck, no one to stop the relentless Red Tide. There are too many Wings with too much to prove and it starts with Yzerman, who has waited 14 years for that skate around the rink. It's close now, so close, the ever-intense captain almost flashed a smile.

"It's exciting, it's a lot of fun, but it's also nerve-wracking," said Yzerman, greeted by a prolonged ovation from fans longing to celebrate. "Things have gone pretty well but you can't afford to relax."

The Wings will get hockey's highest prize because they're loaded with

Flyers captain Eric Lindros feels the sting of the Cup slipping away after a 6-1 defeat in Game 3.

---

players talented and poised, driven by all the emotions — revenge, redemption, respect.

Fedorov? It was said he was too laid-back, didn't care enough about the Cup. It was a rap ridiculously leveled on Russian players, and Fedorov, with three goals in the series and eight in the playoffs, has refuted plenty with perhaps the best all-around hockey of his career.

Vernon? The general in net just will not blink at the huge Flyers. A fan held up a sign for the once-maligned goalie that read simply, "Vernon — I apologize." With the victory, Vernon all but clinched another year on his contract and sealed his standing in Wings lore.

Shanahan? He has scored big goals, has led with emotion and elbows, and in this series, he has matched Philly's overrated toughness.

Scotty Bowman? He came here four seasons ago, suffered three humbling losses in the playoffs, adapted and retooled his team and is poised to deliver the goods.

Of course, before Bowman and his players accept any praise, they do have that little formality.

"We're three-fourths of the way there, that's the way I look at it," Bowman said. "I told the players to enjoy the win for five minutes, then start thinking about the next game."

This was the danger game for the Wings because a Philadelphia victory could have turned the series. But the Wings and their fans aren't

squandering any more time. As the Flyers were introduced before the game, the fans drowned out P.A. announcer Bud Lynch with chants of "Let's Go Red Wings!"

The Wings have no discernible nerves now and nothing to fear, not even Eric Lindros. The Big Red Machine is revved and the only thing that can slow it is overconfidence or a sudden spate of misfortune.

"We've been good all year at learning from past disappointments and turning them into positives," Darren McCarty said. "We were up 3-1 and lost to Colorado, so we're going to get ready for the game of our lives."

Really, this is about persistence and patience now, which seem like different qualities, but not for the Wings.

Ron Hextall continued to crack under the Wings' relentless pressure.

They're patient enough to wait for their chances and their moment, persistent enough to create those chances, to demand that moment.

Even when Philadelphia grabbed a 1-0 lead, the Wings forced the play and didn't give the Flyers a chance to settle into a defensive shell. Not that it's possible to form a defensive shell when you've got a cracked shell in net. Hextall seems like a nice enough guy, but when he stops a puck these days, it's an accident.

You got the feeling early the only way the Wings could lose was if they gave it away. And in a shaky first period, they gave the Flyers four power plays, including a two-man advantage for 1:20. The Wings held firm, largely due to Yzerman's diligent penalty-killing, and when the Flyers failed, the wind and the will left them. The Wings — patiently, persistently — began to hammer.

It keeps coming back to the captain, exactly how it should be. He brought the franchise this far, he might as well push it the rest of the way. Two minutes after John LeClair provided the Flyers' first lead of the series, Yzerman took a quick pass from Vyacheslav Kozlov and fired it through the yawning gap between Hextall's legs.

Barely two minutes later, another Flyer giveaway led to another Detroit breakaway. We understand Philadelphia is the City of Brotherly Love, but really, the outpouring of compassion is startling. Karl Dykhuis lost the puck, Fedorov scooped it up and

Doug Brown and the Wings celebrate Game 3 victory after knocking Philly silly.

took a few strides before flipping a wrister past Hextall for a 2-1 lead.

Philly's weak two-man advantage followed and the Wings proceeded to take the game as if it was the clincher, swarming and smothering the Flyers. Lapointe, Mr. Feisty, grabbed the puck as he exited the penalty box and broke in alone. He fired it off the right post but — ah, persistence — immediately planted himself in front, await-ed a beautiful pass from Doug Brown and beat Hextall to make it 3-1.

"We have to find a way to stop the bleeding, this is an embarrassment," said distraught Flyers coach Terry Murray, who must know now that the Flyers are horribly flawed, and the Wings sense the kill. We have seen it so many times, with 13 victories in their last 15 games. They're all about business, never let up, keep shooting until you see the dead in their eyes.

Shine the Cup and clear the mantle. After 42 years for the franchise, 14 years for the captain, the wait is down to three periods. We expect the Flyers to show up Saturday night, although we're not sure why.

They're merely the wait staff at the biggest party, four decades in the planning and the dreaming, three periods from popping the corks and the ghosts.

NO DROUGHT ABOUT IT: WINGS SKATE AWAY WITH CUP

Yzerman Realizes City's Dream – And His – with Sweep

By Bob Wojnowski

The Detroit News

At the end of the longest wait, after the magical goal by Darren McCarty and the splendid goaltending by Mike Vernon and the nightlong release of emotions raw and real, there was only one more thing to do, and only one person to do it.

After the longest wait, the longest skate. Captain Steve Yzerman finally hoisted the Stanley Cup on Saturday night, and as he skated, starting at center ice, slowly toward one goal, then to the other, he shook the silver trophy again and again, perhaps to make sure it was real. Around the rink he went, raising the Cup to every section, every fan, shaking loose the years of disappointment, and the noise will ring forever.

This was a 41-year drought that had become the singular obsession of a city, a team and a man. The wait is over, the weight is lifted, the nightmares end.

"Sometimes you hold your

FLYERS

1

_____

RED WINGS

2

Detroit,
June 7, 1997

dreams way out there and you wonder if it can ever be as good as you dream," Yzerman said. "It was almost like I wanted to sit back and watch it all and not miss a minute of it."

And those repeated shakes of the Cup?

Yzerman smiled.

"The thing was getting heavy. My arms were giving out."

They were the only parts that ever gave out, as Yzerman's passion sparked a franchise and took it where it hadn't been since 1955. The captain had a cause, and this morning, the Red Wings have the Cup, and sometime around mid-July, the Philadelphia Flyers might recognize what hit them. Spurred by emotion and talent and the relentless red tide of history, the Wings skated through all barriers and took the trophy they had to have.

They won it the only way they could, with contributions from every man on the roster, with Vernon stopping every Philadelphia foray, with all four lines and every defensemen

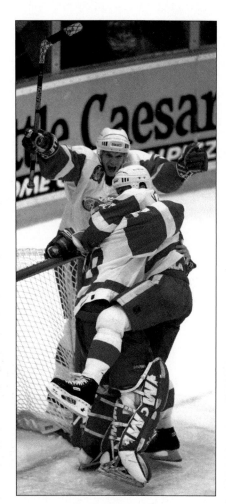

Goalie Mike Vernon and the Wings end the frustration and begin the jubilation as Stanley Cup champions.

making plays when they had to be made. There was Nicklas Lidstrom, the quiet blue-liner, breaking the tension and the scoreless tie late in the first period with a vicious slap shot. There was McCarty, perhaps the team's most underrated player, grabbing the puck and faking defenseman Janne Niinimaa and then faking goalie Ron Hextall and then sprawling to the ice as he scored.

That was the prettiest snapshot from the Wings' 2-1 victory that officially broomed the Flyers, and it was framed by players so determined and dominant, it was scary. Vernon, the playoff MVP, was the man who made the important plays on this night,

stopping 26 shots and capping a phenomenal playoff run. Scotty Bowman was the general behind the bench, making history by winning his seventh Cup with his third franchise, something no one has ever done.

When it was over, the 63-year-old legend donned skates and took a spin with the Cup himself, something else he had never done.

"I always wanted to be an NHL player and skate with the Cup, and you never know how many chances you'll get," he said. "So I figured I'd go for it. It was pretty heavy, but light, too."

If Bowman was the man with the whip, the captain was the guy who

kept it all together, who stood up and spoke when necessary, who was always there, through the lean years and mean years, when he was the only commodity this franchise had.

Now, Yzerman is surrounded by the finest collection of hockey players in the world, and although his scoring role has diminished, his impact never did. It's funny, when he finally gets to smile the broadest, he's missing a tooth, the second dislodging of his career. He gave sweat and blood and teeth and this is why he stayed all these years, 14 in all, through disappointment after disappointment, injury after injury, trade rumor after trade rumor, to take that skate.

He needed a prodding from Brendan Shanahan to begin the longest skate, and when he was done, he handed the Cup to Slava Fetisov and Igor Larionov, the two Russian legends.

"I kind of wanted to do it as a team," Yzerman said, "but it was kind of neat to do it alone."

These Wings did nothing alone, but the "Ste-vie! Ste-vie!" chants will ring the longest, and finally, the cheering wasn't a sentimental gesture for hard work in troubled times, but appreciation for taking a championship team the final step.

Yzerman is the symbol, the lasting image, but he's not a singular star, and that's what makes these Wings unique. They have so many viable components, from the power-skating Sergei Fedorov, to the playmaking Larionov,

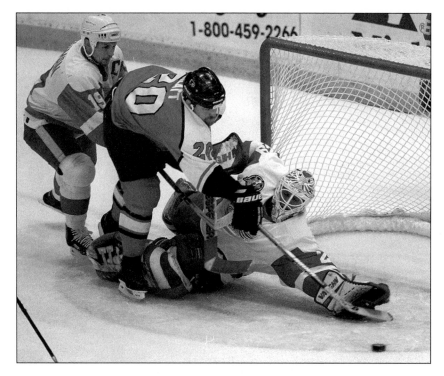

Mike Vernon, the Wings' goalie throughout the playoffs, stopped 26 shots in Game 4 and won the Conn Smythe Award as playoff MVP.

Darren McCarty's beautiful goal clinched Game 4, and he then partied with Joe Louis Arena fans.

to the powerful Shanahan, to big-bodied bangers such as McCarty, Martin Lapointe, Kirk Maltby and Joey Kocur. They have punch along the blue line with Nicklas Lidstrom and Vladimir Konstantinov and savvy veterans in Larry Murphy and Fetisov.

This is a team with so many factions on the ice, few off it. And make no mistake. It was bonded by that March 26 game against Colorado, when McCarty did what he had to do, pounding the life out of Claude Lemieux, pounding it into the Wings.

The Wings had a cause, just like the captain. They erased the stink of their playoff humblings and convinced themselves something special was possible. Now, no more questions, no more sad explanations. No more reminiscing about the good

ol' days when the Wings won all those championships back in the 1950's. The good ol' days are now, resurrected by a team that could not, would not be denied.

Grab a broom and sweep out the old nightmares. Stanley finally came home, delivered by a captain with a cause, and a team that finally found its way.

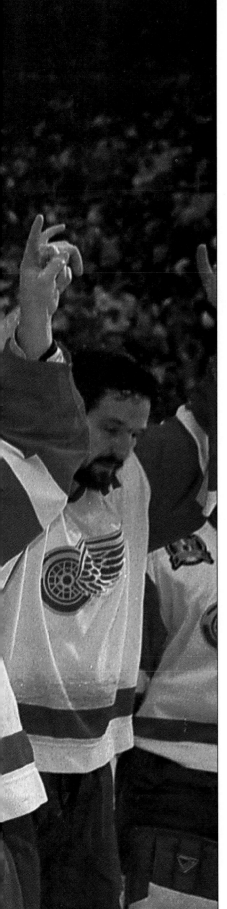

Yzerman Not Loud But Definitely Proud as Wings' Leader

The Quiet Captain Silences His Critics

By Jerry Green
The Detroit News

And then it happened. The guardians, wearing white gloves, opened the strong box that protected the 104-year-old Stanley Cup. The trophy was set, gleaming in the bright lights, onto the table at center ice. And Steve Yzerman, the Captain, skated over to receive it.

At last, long last.

The confetti floated from the rafters. The Red Wings were Stanley Cup champions, for the first time since 1955, 10 years before Yzerman was born. They had swept the Philadelphia Flyers in four games, with sheer ice control, poise, discipline.

Steve Yzerman finally gets his chance to put the Cup overhead.

Yzerman hesitated with the Cup, uncertain. And then he raised it toward his teammates and the cheering multitudes. He caressed it and put it above his head again, pumped it upward in triumph. And then he skated around the ice at Joe Louis Arena in the captain's championship lap.

It was a ritual he knew well. He had watched, in envy, for years as Wayne Gretzky and Mario Lemieux and Mark Messier and Joe Sakic, captains of other conquering teams, had taken the Cup on its annual tour around the rink.

"As long as I could remember, since I was 5 years old, I watched the Stanley Cup, I've stayed up, made a point of watching it presented, watched the celebration in the locker room, and always dreamed that maybe I'd get there," Yzerman said.

"But ... and sometimes you wonder if you'll ever get there. So I guess, as the game was going on, and when we finally won, it's almost like I wanted to sit back and watch the whole thing and not miss a minute of it, and not forget any of it. I don't know if it can ever be as good as the dream, but I'd rather sit back and just watch everybody. I don't want to miss any of it."

Steve Yzerman is a quiet captain. He keeps his emotions harnessed. He seldom shows jubilation, except when he lifts his hockey stick and smiles after scoring a goal. He joined

Yzerman seized the moment in the playoffs, helping the Wings overcome early struggles against the Blues.

the Red Wings when he was 18. At 21, he was captain of the team. He has suffered the indignity of trade rumors, injury, defeat.

And now, at the end of his 14th season, he had his grip on the Stanley Cup. At last. He began his solo skate, slowly, searching into the grandstands, into the multitudes.

"I was looking for my parents," he said. "And then I was looking for my wife in the corner."

He toured to the far side of the rink, to the roar of the crowd, as his

Yzerman encountered years of playoff frustrations against the likes of Mark Messier and the Edmonton Oilers.

team waited for him to return.

"The thing was getting heavy," Yzerman said. "My arms were giving out."

He skated around and handed the Cup to Slava Fetisov, one of the Red Wings' celebrated and sometimes maligned, Russian Five. Fetisov is pushing 40, a defenseman whose craggy face displayed a series of stick scars from more than 20 years of high-level hockey wars. He had won Olympic and world championships for the Soviet Union. He played for the renowned Red Army team, or CSKA, in Moscow. Then with bitterness, he broke with the Red Army team and led the stream of Russian hockey defectors to North America — just as communism collapsed and the Soviet Union fragmented.

It was to Fetisov that Captain Yzerman handed the trophy to begin the tradition in which every player has his turn to hoist, kiss and cherish the Cup. Fetisov placed one side of the Cup into the hands of Igor Larionov, his 36-year-old teammate with the Red Army and the Red Wings. They skated in tandem with the Cup.

Through the years of the Red Wings' failures to win, critics had faulted the Russians for not comprehending the spirit of the Stanley Cup.

"As far as giving it to Slava," said Yzerman, "the last couple of days — you try not to think about anything but the game, you've got a million things running through your mind, and I got caught up with who should I hand the Cup off to?

"I thought of a few different players. Slava jumped to my mind because of what he's done. He and Igor, what kind of guys they are. I really respect them, what they've done and how they've handled

Although his goal production has decreased with age, Yzerman still was an integral scorer in the Wings' offense.

themselves, and they set an example in their work ethic and their attitude for the young Russian players. And they've been real leaders on our team.

"I don't know if Slava's coming back next year or not. But after the great career he's had I wanted him to get the trophy. He's done everything in the world of hockey, and this is the most important thing, so I wanted to give it to him."

The symbolism was captured. Steve Yzerman, through the years, had been a captain criticized often for not being loud or sufficiently vocal in his leadership. He explained so often that he stresses leadership by example.

Part of his quiet front is shyness. Part of it is modesty. He was born in British Columbia, grew up in Nepean, Ontario, in suburban Ottawa. He was raised well in citizenship. He was raised well in hockey.

Seldom has he rebuked his teammates. But he did in the first round of the 1997 playoffs, when they were deadlocked after a 4-0 loss to St. Louis. He stood up and challenged his team, urging them to start producing. He included himself in the criticism.

Seldom has he jabbed at a player. But in the 1997 series with Colorado, Sergei Fedorov rode into the boards, damaging his ribs. Fedorov could barely breath. He was assisted to the dressing room. He was considered done for the game. Yzerman approached him after the first period: "Sergei, we need you." Fedorov soon returned. He was brilliant when he got back. He scored the winning goal that eliminated the Avalanche.

Seldom has he engaged in hockey's rough stuff, the fighting. But one night, years ago when a brawl broke out, Yzerman was seen punching the Canadiens' Bobby Smith in a corner of the Forum.

It is leadership.

And as Yzerman led, each of the Red Wings did his bit with the Stanley Cup. Even Scotty Bowman, with his seventh Stanley Cup championship as a coach, put on his skates to ride with the trophy. Then the Cup was taken from the ice. It was transported into the Red Wings dressing room, into the back, where on the stationary bikes Yzerman had pedaled for hours, days, restrengthening muscle from his various injuries.

The bandwagon rolled into the champions' dressing room soon after the Cup. Folks who had recently discovered that water freezes at 32 degrees Fahrenheit to form ice poured into the room. It was jammed, sweltering from the TV lights, champagne spraying around the room, drenching the red shirts and dresses of the interlopers.

Yzerman stood out front among the crowd. His face was soaked with sweat. He had the very beginnings of another playoff goatee on his chin and cheeks. He had stripped off his No. 19 jersey with the captain's C on the left front shoulder. He wore a cap that read: "Stanley Cup CHAMPS." And he patiently endeavored to deliver the feelings of his past frustrations to the media marvels who were about to reach him. Mostly, he expressed relief — that it was his turn and he was relishing it.

"I love this team," he said.

"I was going to feel all this different stuff. It happened too quick. When I started playing as a kid, I dreamed of the NHL and the Stanley

Cup. But it was filled with a lot of disappointments ... a lot of tough losses. I think I'm a better player for it.

"The hardest part is sitting around waiting. I can usually sleep the afternoon before a game. I couldn't today. I just wanted to be left alone. Let's get on the ice and play.

"We've had some disappointments and we've broken people's hearts. People would always say, as good as you are, you didn't win the Cup.

"Now people can't say that."

Yzerman spoke as the bedlam went on around him. It was after midnight, early Sunday morning. Brendan Shanahan came up and spoke words into Yzerman's ear. Shanahan was still dressed in full game regalia, his No. 14 jersey, his ice skates.

A half-dozen mini tape recorders nearly brushed Yzerman's whiskers. Some reporters stood in the second circle around him, scratching his words into their notebooks. Fans pushed in.

They, the hockey fans, are passionate people. In Detroit, they are vigorously devoted to their team. They are fickle, of course. In the few years past they had rabidly cheered the Red Wings when they had hugely successful regular seasons, then were defeated in the playoffs. They felt disgraced when the Red Wings went out in the first round to the ancient-rival Maple Leafs one year, then the upstart San Jose Sharks the next. They bled and cursed when

Yzerman was criticized for the Wings' previous playoff problems. "The last five years, you didn't want to be recognized," he said.

the Red Wings reached the Stanley Cup Finals for the first time in 29 years in 1995, then were swept in four games by the New Jersey Devils. And they vilified their team when the Red Wings were defeated in 1996 in the bitter Western Conference final series by the hated Colorado Avalanche.

Yzerman was among those condemned by anonymous fans, callers to sports talk shows: "He never turns up for the playoffs." "He's always hurt."

Uncontrolled rumors abounded that the Red Wings would trade him.

"The last five years, you didn't want to be recognized," Yzerman said to his audience. "I put a hat on, glasses on. You don't want people to recognize you.

"A couple of years ago I went to Las Vegas after the playoffs. I don't remember which year. I was at the craps table. Two old guys from Windsor came by and saw me. They said, 'You don't want to play at this table. There's no luck at this table.'"

About that time, Yzerman sat with a single reporter in a rare interview, speaking his inner feelings.

"Yeah, always," he said about watching the Stanley Cup presentation ceremony on television in his home in suburban Detroit each spring. "You're driving down the road and some song comes on the radio and you're thinking about it. I've always thought about that, every year.

"Every year I've always tried, no matter what I'm doing, no matter what I've seen or missed of the playoffs, I always try to make a point of seeing the final game — or the end of the final game — because I enjoy seeing the Stanley Cup presented.

"I enjoy seeing the Super Bowl, or the world championship in baseball or basketball.

"I like seeing the finish part. Yeah, I think everybody, whatever they dream of, always pictures it the same way.

Yzerman, never the vocal type as a bench leader, preferred to lead the Wings by example.

"I've got friends who've won the Cup, and it's interesting to see people when they win and how they react. To see them in the summer and ask what it was like. Just to see what it's like ...

"Very envious ...

"I found that the last couple of years, as the hype and expectation for our team has grown, there are setbacks along the way. And although they seem the end of the world at the time, you survive, improve and improve, and at some point, you get to reach your goal.

"But every year, as we've kind of faded in the playoffs, it grows a little more imperative — I guess in my mind — to accomplish what you want to accomplish."

Now, after 14 years, mature at 32,

he had accomplished what he wanted to accomplish. He did it as a player who had been required to adjust his style, make alternate use of his skills.

Through his first 10 seasons in Detroit, Yzerman's primary function was to score goals. He became one of the more prolific scorers in the NHL. He ranked in stature with Gretzky and Lemieux. He became regarded as the second greatest offensive player in the franchise's history, after only Gordie Howe. In 1988-89, Yzerman scored 65 goals. In other seasons, he scored 62, 58, 51 and 50 goals. Howe had 49 in his best goal-scoring season.

The sport, of course, was different when Howe played it. Schedules were shorter. There were six teams,

Despite numerous trade rumors, especially those circulating in his hometown of Ottawa, Yzerman remained the Wings' captain.

all skilled. Expansion created a 26-team league, diluted in talent.

But Howe had won the Stanley Cup four times.

When Bowman became the Red Wings' coach in 1993, one of his earliest machinations was to try to recreate Yzerman. Bowman wanted a fast, slick defensive forward, one adept at forechecking. Yzerman never complained. But he did not thrill to the change.

He still scored, but never with the production of the earlier years. So the critics harped. The trade rumors proliferated.

There had been reports that he would be traded after the Red Wings lost in the playoffs in 1994 to San Jose. They vanished without merit.

But such rumors were wildly pounced upon after the Jersey sweep for the Cup in 1995. The Ottawa Senators made an overture for Yzerman. He was a hometown player. They had a general manager, Randy Sexton, who was on the cusp, trying to salvage his job. The Senators had a new rink and needed a name player to lure fans inside. Rumors were floated in Ottawa, printed as a done deal. They were refloated in Detroit.

Yzerman fretted. The Senators were an expansion team with a dubious future. They were mismanaged.

The trade rumors proliferated. Out of character, at a practice session before the season opened in 1995,

Yzerman lost his temper. He threw his stick. He barked at the media.

As it turned out, he wasn't traded. The rumors had slammed out of control, based on Ottawa's wishful thinking. Two high-echelon sources on the Red Wings confirmed that an Yzerman trade was never seriously close. Jimmy Devellano, a Detroit club vice-president, said the Red Wings had stacked the price so high for Yzerman that the Senators could never afford to make such a deal.

Two things happened in the aftermath.

Yzerman mused about the media, still miffed.

"Don't they have any accountability?" he said one day.

The second thing that happened was that Mike Ilitch, the club owner, signed him to a contract that bound him to the Red Wings for the duration of his career. It would pay $17.5 million over four seasons, and guaranteed a front-office job when Yzerman retired as a player.

That night, Yzerman celebrated. He had a goal and three assists.

Perhaps, of all the goals he has scored — 539 in the regular season and and 46 in the playoffs — his finest, his most sensational was in the 1996 playoffs. A seven-game struggle with the St. Louis Blues went into double overtime. Yzerman ended it with a blazing shot. He spun around behind the net with all his teammates on top of him, thumping his back.

That would be surpassed by the goal he scored against the Avalanche in the second game of the 1997 Western Conference finals. The Red Wings had lost the first game and had trailed, 2-0, in the second. Quickly, they were in position for another disappointment. Detroit tied it. Yzerman set up Fedorov for the tying goal.

With four minutes left, Yzerman got the puck in the Detroit zone, sped through center, around the Colorado defense. From behind the net he shoved the puck at goalie Patrick Roy. It went in off Roy's leg. It would become the most vital goal of Yzerman's 14 seasons in Detroit.

It turned around the series. From then on, the Red Wings were dominant against Colorado — losing only one more game — and over Philadelphia — losing none. Yzerman had another key goal in the first game of the Finals, the long-distance shot that doomed the Flyers.

Several years ago, the Canadiens signed Patrick Roy to a contract paying $4 million a season. To justify such a sum at that time, Serge Savard, then Canadiens' general manager, explained to Montreal reporters that Roy had won Stanley Cups, "a guy like Yzerman has never won anything."

But now it has happened. The Captain has his Cup.

In 14 seasons as a Red Wing, Yzerman has had many moments in the spotlight.

PHOTO CREDITS